Numbers

*Not yet published as of this printing.

BIBLE STUDY COMMENTARY

Numbers

F. B. HUEY, JR.

Lamplighter Books Grand Rapids, Michigan
Zondervan Publishing House

NUMBERS: BIBLE STUDY COMMENTARY
Copyright © 1981 by The Zondervan Corporation
Grand Rapids, Michigan

Lamplighter Books are published by Zondervan
Publishing House, 1415 Lake Drive, S.E.,
Grand Rapids, Michigan 49506

Library of Congress Cataloging in Publication Data

Huey, F. B., 1925–
    Numbers, Bible study commentary.

    Bibliography: p.
    1. Bible.   O.T.   Numbers—Commentaries.   I. Title.
BS1265.3.H8   222'.1407   81-21905
ISBN 0-310-36073-0   AACR2

Printed in the United States of America

88 89 90 91 92 93 / CH / 10 9 8 7 6 5 4 3

Contents

Introduction

A. Importance of the Book of Numbers

Well-intentioned Bible students who determine to read straight through the Bible frequently find the initial joy that is experienced in reading Genesis does not last. They are soon exhausted by Exodus, lost in Leviticus, numbed by Numbers, and done in by Deuteronomy! They return to John in the New Testament and never again attempt the study of the Old Testament, with the possible exception of the Psalms.

Such an experience is unfortunate, for without a good grasp of the Pentateuch (the first five books of the Old Testament), the serious Bible student never fully understands much of the New Testament. Atonement, blood sacrifice, holiness, election, and righteousness are only a few of the New Testament doctrines that find their origin in the Old Testament. A firm resolution to study the Pentateuch, though it may not be easy reading at first, will be rewarded by understanding and spiritual growth.

The Book of Numbers is an important part of the Old Testament. It is the major source for the experiences of the Israelites during their journey from Mount Sinai to the Promised Land. It explains why a journey that should have taken two weeks at most required forty years to complete. It describes the one sin that Moses committed during the entire forty years that prevented him from entering Canaan with his people. It contains fascinating narratives, such as the rebellion of Korah, Balaam's attempts to curse the Israelites, and the visit of fiery serpents (that became the basis of an utterance concerning Jesus in John 3:14). It includes some unusual regulations, such as the ordeal of jealousy, the Nazirite vow, and vows made by women.

Perhaps the most important lessons of the book are that God acts for the ultimate good of His people, demands obedience at all times, and is able to accomplish His purposes in spite of human sins. A careful study of Numbers will convince the reader that "all Scripture is God-breathed and is useful" (2 Tim. 3:16).[1]

B. Name of the Book

It was common practice in the ancient Near East to name a book after its first word or first significant phrase. In the Hebrew Bible the Book of Numbers is called "and he spoke" (the first word in Hebrew) or "in the desert" (the fifth but first significant word). The Septuagint (the first translation into Greek) called it *Arithmoi* (meaning "Numbers," a reference to the censuses that are prominent in the book). The Latin Vulgate called it *Numeri*, from which the English title, Numbers, comes.

However, none of the titles by which the book is known adequately describes its content, which is largely about the years spent by the Israelites in the desert before finally reaching their destination. It has been facetiously called the "Book of Complaints" because it records numerous complaints and acts of disobedience and rebellion on the part of the Israelites, who had so recently been delivered from slavery in Egypt.

C. Authorship

For almost 1,800 years of the Christian era, few doubts were expressed about the Mosaic authorship of the Pentateuch. However, under the impact of the views of Julius Wellhausen and other critical scholars of the nineteenth century, all but the most conservative biblical scholars abandoned belief in Mosaic authorship early in the twentieth century.

Conservative scholars who continue to support Mosaic authorship argue that (1) Jesus Himself affirmed that Moses wrote the books (e.g., Mark 10:4–5; Luke 24:44; John 5:46–47); (2) Moses was qualified by background and education to write the books; (3) claims for Mosaic authorship are found in the Pentateuch (e.g., Exod. 17:14; 24:4; 34:27–28; Num. 33:2; Deut. 31:9, 22, 24–26); (4) the oldest Jewish

---

[1]Unless otherwise indicated, all Scriptures quoted in this book are from the New International Version. Wherever a Scripture reference is found without the name of the book, it is from the Book of Numbers, e.g., 22:3 means Numbers 22:3.

traditions hold that Moses was the author; and (5) archaeology has confirmed the accuracy of events, names, and customs that are found in the Pentateuch, implying that the author did not write hundreds of years after the events recorded there.

Questions especially pertinent to Mosaic authorship of Numbers include: (1) Why is Moses always referred to in the third person? (2) Would Moses have written Numbers 12:3 about himself? (3) Does the specific acknowledgment of copied sources (21:14, 27) suggest that other sources were used? (4) How does one explain different writing styles, duplications, and other anomalies in this and the other books of the Pentateuch?[2]

Though it is unlikely that conservative and liberal scholars will ever agree on Mosaic authorship, there is presently a growing conviction that the tradition of Mosaic authorship is not a fabrication; and even the most liberal scholars concede that some parts of the Pentateuch can be traced to Moses. However, all disputes among scholars over Mosaic authorship become secondary if we agree that Numbers, or any other book of the Bible, was written under the inspiration of the Spirit of God. The Reformer, John Calvin, spoke pointedly to the debate when he said, "God is the real author."

D. The Question of the Number of Israelites

The question most frequently raised in connection with the Book of Numbers concerns the number of people involved in the journey from Egypt to Canaan. The total number of men twenty years of age or more and fit for military service in the first census totaled 603,550 (1:46; cf. Exod. 12:37). The second census almost forty years later revealed approximately the same number (26:51). By adding men not eligible for military service, women, and children, the total would easily become more than two million people. The logistics of moving such a large number through a desert region, maintaining order and communication as they traveled, providing food for them, crossing the Red Sea in one day (Exod. 14:21–22, 30), and taking a census in one day (Num. 1:18) are questions that cannot be ignored.

---

[2]For a representative defense of traditional Mosaic authorship of the Pentateuch, see J. W. Wenham, "Moses and the Pentateuch," in *The New Bible Commentary Revised*, ed. D. Guthrie et al. (Grand Rapids: Wm. B. Eerdmans Publishing Company, 1970), pp. 41–43. For a history of Pentateuchal criticism, see Elmer B. Smick, "Pentateuch," in *The Zondervan Pictorial Encyclopedia of the Bible*, ed. Merrill C. Tenney (Grand Rapids: Zondervan Publishing House, 1975), 4:674–92.

A variety of solutions have been proposed to explain the numbers involved in the Exodus journey. They include the following: (1) It is better to accept the numbers literally in spite of the problems created because an admission of inaccuracy in one part of the Bible opens all parts to the same charge; it is also possible that evidence not yet available will clarify and support the biblical numbers. (2) The entire story of the Exodus should be seen as an etiological legend written much later than the events. It is a kind of epic literary composition written to explain the origin of the Israelite nation; therefore, there is no necessity to be concerned about historical inaccuracies. This is the position of most liberal scholars, who arbitrarily reduce the total number to a few thousand who left Egypt and justify the reduction by Deuteronomy 7:7. (3) Instead of understanding the Hebrew word *'elep* to mean "thousand," it should be taken to mean "a military unit" (another meaning of the word); thus, e.g., 46,500 (1:21) becomes 46 military units totaling 500 men. (4) The Hebrew word cited in (3) means "tribal chieftain" or "leader" (a meaning of the word gained by changing its vowels); thus, e.g., 46,500 (1:21) becomes 46 chieftains over 500 warriors. (5) It is best to view the census figures as part of a document that somehow became separated from David's census (2 Sam. 24:1–9). (6) The numbers are to be taken as figurative (as is much language in the Old Testament); they express through exaggeration the power and importance of the covenant people known as Israel (cf. 1 Sam. 18:7). (7) The expositor should use gematria (finding hidden meaning through numerical equivalents of Hebrew letters); thus he discovers that 603,550 (1:46) means "the sum of all . . . the children of Israel" (1:2 KJV).[3]

It should be noted that any attempt to reduce the number of people creates other problems. If only a few thousand were involved in the Exodus, why were the Egyptians afraid of them and why did they oppress them to reduce their numbers (Exod. 1:9)? Why did the Israelites have such concern about food supplies (Exod. 16:2–3)? Why were the burdens of settling their disputes so time-consuming for Moses (Exod. 18:13–23)? Why were the Moabites terrified of them (22:3)? Since no single solution has commended itself to a majority of

---

[3]For an explanation of gematria see Georg Fohrer, *Introduction to the Old Testament*, trans. David E. Green (Nashville/New York: Abingdon Press, 1968), p. 184; John J. Davis, *Biblical Numerology: A Basic Study of the Use of Numbers in the Bible* (Grand Rapids: Baker Book House, 1968), pp. 126–49.

scholars, we should be on guard that any attempt to reduce the numbers may solve some problems but at the same time will create others. Whatever the exact number may have been, God's constant guidance and providence were required to bring Israel into the Promised Land.

E. Outline of the Book

The Book of Numbers may be divided into three major parts that correspond with the stages of the Israelites' journey from Mount Sinai to the border of the Promised Land: Part One: Preparations for the Departure From Sinai (chaps. 1:1–10:10); Part Two: The Journey From Sinai to Moab (chaps. 10:11–21:35); Part Three: Events on the Plains of Moab (chaps. 22–36). These major divisions are further subdivided, and the chapter divisions of the book follow these subdivisions.

Part One: Preparations for the Departure From Sinai (1:1–10:10)
  Chapter 1: Numbering and Arrangement of the Tribes (1:1–4:49)
    A. The first census (1:1–54)
      1. Plans for the census (1:1–16)
      2. The census by tribes (1:17–46)
      3. Duties of the Levites (1:47–54)
    B. Organization of the people for the journey (2:1–34)
      1. Position in camp (2:1–33)
        a) The east side (2:1–9)
        b) The south side (2:10–17)
        c) The west side (2:18–24)
        d) The north side (2:25–33)
      2. Position en route (2:34)
    C. Organization of the priests (3:1–51)
      1. The sons of Aaron (3:1–4)
      2. Duties of the Levites (3:5–10)
      3. Significance of the Levites (3:11–13)
      4. Census of the Levites (3:14–39)
      5. Census and redemption of the firstborn males (3:40–51)
    D. Census and duties of the Levites (4:1–49)
      1. Duties of the Kohathites (4:1–20)
      2. Duties of the Gershonites (4:21–28)
      3. Duties of the Merarites (4:29–33)
      4. The numbering of the Levites (4:34–49)

Chapter 4: The Wanderings in the Desert—I (13:1–15:41)
   A. The twelve spies (13:1–33)
        1. Appointment of the spies (13:1–16)
        2. Moses' instructions to the spies (13:17–20)
        3. The investigation and report of the spies (13:21–29)
        4. The spies' recommendation (13:30–33)
   B. The reaction to the spies' report (14:1–45)
        1. The people's complaint (14:1–4)
        2. The appeal of Joshua and Caleb (14:5–9)
        3. God's anger (14:10–12)
        4. Moses' intercession (14:13–19)
        5. God's response (14:20–35)
        6. Judgment on the spies (14:36–38)
        7. Defeat by the Amalekites and Canaanites (14:39–45)
   C. Additional laws and regulations (15:1–41)
        1. Grain offerings and drink offerings (15:1–16)
        2. An offering of the first of the ground meal (15:17–21)
        3. Atonement for unintentional sins (15:22–31)
        4. Punishment for work on the Sabbath (15:32–36)
        5. Tassels on the garments (15:37–41)
Chapter 5: The Wanderings in the Desert—II (16:1–19:22)
   A. Rebellion among the people (16:1–50)
        1. Leaders of the rebellion (16:1–2)
        2. Korah's rebellion (16:3–11)
        3. The rebellion of Dathan and Abiram (16:12–14)
        4. Punishment of the rebels (16:15–35)
        5. A sign for the people (16:36–40)
        6. Punishment of the people (16:41–50)
   B. The budding of Aaron's rod (17:1–13)
   C. Wages and duties of the priests and Levites (18:1–32)
        1. Duties (18:1–7)
        2. Offerings due the priests (18:8–20)
        3. The tithe for the Levites (18:21–24)
        4. Additional payment to the priests (18:25–32)
   D. The rite of the red heifer (19:1–22)
        1. Instructions for slaughter of the heifer (19:1–10)
        2. Purification for defilement by a corpse (19:11–19)
        3. Punishment for ignoring the purification law (19:20–22)

Chapter 6: The Journey From Paran to Moab (20:1–21:35)
  A. The end of the desert wanderings (20:1–29)
    1. The death of Miriam (20:1)
    2. The people's complaint for water (20:2–9)
    3. Striking of the rock (20:10–13)
    4. Request for passage through Edom denied (20:14–21)
    5. The death of Aaron (20:22–29)
  B. Final events before reaching Moab (21:1–35)
    1. Defeat of the king of Arad (21:1–3)
    2. The fiery serpents (21:4–9)
    3. The journey from Oboth to Pisgah (21:10–20)
    4. Encounter with Sihon, king of the Amorites (21:21–30)
    5. Encounter with Og, king of Bashan (21:31–35)

Part Three: Events on the Plains of Moab (22:1–36:13)
  Chapter 7: The Story of Balaam (22:1–24:25)
    A. Balak and Balaam (22:1–40)
      1. Moab's fear of Israel (22:1–6)
      2. Balak's first request thwarted (22:7–14)
      3. Balak's second request (22:15–20)
      4. Balaam and his donkey (22:21–35)
      5. Balaam's meeting with Balak (22:36–40)
    B. The oracles of Balaam (22:41–24:25)
      1. The first oracle about Israel (22:41–23:12)
      2. The second oracle about Israel (23:13–26)
      3. The third oracle about Israel (23:27–24:13)
      4. Other oracles (24:14–25)
  Chapter 8: A Second Census and Other Regulations (25:1–30:16)
    A. Consequences of foreign entanglements (25:1–18)
      1. Apostasy at Peor (25:1–5)
      2. The zeal of Phinehas (25:6–18)
    B. The second census (26:1–65)
      1. Plans for the census (26:1–4)
      2. The census taken by tribes (26:5–51)
      3. Regulations for land inheritance (26:52–56)
      4. Census of the Levites (26:57–62)
      5. The only survivors of the desert (26:63–65)
    C. Inheritance laws for daughters (27:1–11)
    D. Appointment of Joshua as Moses' successor (27:12–23)

PART ONE: *Preparations for the Departure From Sinai*

Chapter 1

Numbering and Arrangement of the Tribes
(Numbers 1:1–4:49)

The Book of Numbers continues where the Book of Leviticus ends. The Israelites were still encamped at Mount Sinai. The covenant with God had been made, the tabernacle built, worship begun, and additional laws and regulations given. Now it was time to prepare for the entrance into the Promised Land, a journey of less than two weeks from where they were encamped.

A. The First Census (1:1–54)

1. Plans for the census (1:1–16)

God spoke to Moses in the Tent of Meeting ("tabernacle of the congregation," KJV) while the Israelites were still in the Desert of Sinai. It was exactly one month since the tabernacle had been erected (1:1; cf. Exod. 40:17). God instructed Moses to take a census (literally, "lift up the head") of all the people by clans and families (1:2). Only the men twenty years of age or more and who were able to fight were to be counted (1:3). One man from each tribe was named to assist Moses and Aaron in the task (1:4–15). Of the twenty-six names of descendants of the sons of Jacob in these verses, thirteen are theophorous, i.e., contain a reference to God. The men chosen to assist were all leaders among their tribes (1:16).

2. The census by tribes (1:17–46)

The census was carried out without delay on the same day (1:18). By means of a formula that is repeated almost without variation, the reader is given the total number of each tribe. The tribe of Levi was not included in this census. However, the number twelve was maintained by counting the tribe of Joseph as two tribes, Ephraim and Manasseh (vv. 32–35). Judah's prominence among the tribes is indicated by its size as the largest tribe (1:27; cf. Gen. 49:8). Manasseh, the smallest tribe (1:35), was one of the larger tribes at the time of the second census (26:34). The total number of men included in the census was 603,550 (1:46; cf. 11:21; Exod. 12:37).[1]

3. Duties of the Levites (1:47–54)

The Levites were not included in the census of the other tribes (1:47–49). The purpose of the census was to determine the number of fighting men; and the Levites, because of their contact with sacred things, could not be warriors. They were assigned the responsibility of the tabernacle and all its furnishings. They were also in charge of its transport, erection, and care. They pitched their tents around the tabernacle to protect it from the approach of an unauthorized person, lest that person be put to death and God's wrath fall on all the people. The other tribes were instructed to set up their tents by divisions, each person in his own camp beside his own standard (1:50–53). The Levitical duties outlined in 1:50–53 are detailed in Numbers 3–4.

B. Organization of the People for the Journey (2:1–34)

For the journey that lay ahead there had to be some orderly plan of arrangement for the tribes both while encamped and while marching, lest there be utter confusion.

1. Position in camp (2:1–33)

The overall plan required that the Israelites camp around the Tent of Meeting at some distance. Each man camped by his own standard with the banners that would identify his family (2:2). Three tribes were to be located on each side with the Levites in the middle between the tabernacle and the other tribes. The whole scene was a vivid reminder of God's presence in the midst of His people.

a) The east side (2:1–9)

The position of the tribes around the tabernacle is given in clockwise order (east, south, west, north). The most important of the three tribes on each side is named first. The names of the tribal leaders in this chapter are the same as those in chapter 1. Judah was given the place of

---

[1]The question of the number of Israelites has been discussed in the Introduction, pp. 9–11.

honor on the east, as the position meant that tribe would be at the head as the tribes traveled. The tribes of Issachar and Zebulun were assigned to the east side with Judah. Altogether, the men fit for military service from these three tribes totaled 186,400 (2:9).

b) *The south side* (2:10–17)

Though the eldest son, Reuben, did not occupy the chief position of honor among the tribes, he was leader of the tribes on the south side. (Cf. Gen. 49:3–12, where Jacob gave the principal blessing to the fourth son, Judah, instead of to one of the first three: Reuben, Simeon, or Levi.) The tribes of Simeon and Gad were assigned to the south side with Reuben. Altogether, the men fit for military service from these three tribes totaled 151,450 (2:16). While traveling, these tribes would follow the tribes of the east side. They in turn were followed by the Levites, who encircled the Tent of Meeting as they carried it (2:17). After them came the tribes who had encamped on the west and north sides. This order allowed the Levites to be in the middle of the tribes, whether marching or camping. However, 10:17–21 places the tabernacle after the first three tribes and the other holy articles after the next three.

c) *The west side* (2:18–24)

The three tribes located on the west side were the descendants of Rachel. Led by the tribe of Ephraim, Manasseh and Benjamin were also assigned to that side. Altogether, the men fit for military service from these three tribes totaled 108,100 (2:24). In the march they set out after the Levites.

d) *The north side* (2:25–33)

Encamped on the north side was the tribe of Dan, and the tribes of Asher and Naphtali were assigned to the north side with Dan. It is of interest to note that these three tribes also settled furthest north in Canaan. Altogether, the men fit for military service from these three tribes totaled 157,600 (2:31). In the march these tribes brought up the rear. Once again the total number of men, excluding the Levites, fit for military service is given as 603,550 (2:32–33).

2. *Position en route* (2:34)

The tribes were organized and placed as the Lord had commanded Moses. They maintained these positions whenever they encamped under their standards and whenever they set out on march. The entire arrangement of the tribes is a picture of God dwelling in the midst of an obedient people with His holiness carefully protected.

C. Organization of the priests (3:1–51)

After dealing with the organization of the secular tribes, the Lord turned His attention to the priestly families. He ordered a census of them and gave them their duties (chaps. 3–4).

1. The sons of Aaron (3:1–4)

Attention in the narrative now turns to the sons of Aaron. It is somewhat unusual to mention Aaron before Moses (3:1). The order is understandable here since the narrative deals only with Aaron's descendants. His firstborn was Nadab, and he had three other sons: Abihu, Eleazar, and Ithamar (3:2; cf. Exod. 6:23). All of them had previously been anointed and ordained (literally, "filled their hands," 3:3; cf. Exod. 29; 30:30).

Brief reference is made to the deaths of Nadab and Abihu when they offered "unauthorized" fire ("strange," KJV; "unholy," RSV; "unlawful," JB; "illicit," NEB; "profane," NAB) before the Lord (3:4; cf. Lev. 10:1–7). The various translations reflect the uncertainty of the nature of their sin. Nadab and Abihu left no children to succeed Aaron as high priest; therefore, the priestly family continued through the descendants of Eleazar and Ithamar (3:4; cf. 1 Chron. 24:1–4), who served during the lifetime of their father (literally, "upon the face/presence of Aaron").

2. Duties of the Levites (3:5–10)

These verses establish the subordination of the Levites to the priests. Genealogically, priests and Levites were related, for they came from a common ancestor, Levi. However, as religious institutions they were entirely and completely distinct. Levites, of course, had to be descended from Levi, as well as the priests; but the essential element of the priesthood was descent from Aaron, who was a descendant of Levi. Priests were not exalted Levites, nor were the Levites degraded priests. The Levites were primarily servants of the priests and the whole community at the tabernacle (3:6–8; cf. Ezek. 44:10–31).[2]

The Levites were "given wholly" (literally, "given, given," 3:9; "especially dedicated," NEB) to Aaron and his sons. In 3:40–45 it is added that they were first given to the Lord (cf. 8:16–19). Only Aaron

---

[2]For another view of the relation between the priests and Levites see R. Abba, "Priests and Levites," in *Interpreter's Dictionary of the Bible*, 4 vols., ed. George Arthur Buttrick et al. (New York/Nashville: Abingdon Press, 1962), 3:876–89; George Buchanan Gray, *A Critical and Exegetical Commentary on Numbers*, The International Critical Commentary (Edinburgh: T. & T. Clark, 1903), pp. 21–26.

and his sons could function as priests. Anyone else who approached the sanctuary would be put to death (3:10; cf. 1 Kings 12:31, where Jeroboam allowed non-Levites to be priests).

3. *Significance of the Levites* (3:11–13)

The Lord told Moses that He was taking the Levites for His service instead of the first male offspring of every Israelite woman (3:11–12). He slew all the firstborn of the Egyptians and at the same time set apart the firstborn Israelites for Himself. All the firstborn belonged to Him. However, instead of taking them for His service, He substituted the Levites (3:12–13; cf. Exod. 13:11–12; 22:29; 34:19–20). In primitive societies the firstborn male child was frequently sacrificed to the deity, but human sacrifice was abhorrent to God. Therefore, He made provision for redemption of the firstborn.[3] The words of the Lord concluded with a solemn "I am the LORD" (3:13), a phrase characteristic of Leviticus 17–26.

4. *Census of the Levites* (3:14–39)

The Levites had not been included in the general census (1:1–46); so God ordered Moses to count every male among them a month old and more by families and clans (3:14–15). Levi had three sons, Gershon, Kohath, and Merari (3:17), whose sons became the heads of the clans named in 3:18–20 (cf. Exod. 6:16–19). One of them, Amram of the Kohathite clan (3:19), was the father of Moses and Aaron (cf. Exod. 6:18, 20).

In a parallel to the census and arrangement of the secular tribes about the tabernacle, the Levites were counted by families and clans. Their position around the tabernacle was also designated. The males of the Gershon clans of Libni and Shimei who were a month old and more totaled 7,500 (3:22; cf. 1 Chron. 23:7; Zech. 12:13). They were to camp on the west side of the tabernacle under the leadership of Eliasaph, son of Lael (3:23–24). They were given the responsibility for the care of the tabernacle and tent, its coverings, the curtain at the entrance to the Tent of Meeting, the curtains of the courtyard, the curtain at the entrance to the courtyard around the tabernacle and altar, and the ropes and everything related to their use (3:25–26; cf. Exod. 26:1–14).

---

[3]For comments on the dedication laws of Exodus 13:1–16 for the firstborn, see F. B. Huey, Jr., *Exodus: Bible Study Commentary* (Grand Rapids: Zondervan Publishing House, 1977), pp. 61–62.

In other words, they were in charge of all that covered and screened the tabernacle, tent, and court. They were not responsible for the structure itself, which was under the care of the Merarites (3:36).

The males a month old and more of the Kohathite clans—the Amramites, Izharites, Hebronites, and Uzzielites—totaled 8,600 (3:27-28; some LXX manuscripts say 8,300; cf. comments on 3:39). They were to camp on the south side of the tabernacle under the leadership of Elizaphan, son of Uzziel (3:29-30). They were responsible for the care of the sanctuary that included the ark, the table of the bread of the Presence ("table of shewbread," KJV), the gold lampstand, the altars, the articles of the sanctuary used in ministering, the curtain, and everything related to their use (3:31).

The duties of the Kohathites set them apart as especially favored among the Levites, perhaps because they included the descendants of Amram, Moses' father. Because their duties placed them in such close contact with the priests, their work was placed under the supervision of Eleazar, eldest surviving son of Aaron and himself a Kohathite (3:32; cf. Exod. 6:18, 20, 23).

The males a month old and more of the Merarite clans of Mahli and Mushi totaled 6,200 (3:33-34; the LXX says 6,050). They were to camp on the north side of the tabernacle under the leadership of Zuriel, son of Abihail (3:35). They were responsible for the frames of the tabernacle, its crossbars, posts, bases, all its equipment, and everything related to their use. They were also in charge of the posts of the surrounding courtyard with their bases, tent pegs, and ropes (3:36-37; cf. Exod. 26:15-30, 32, 37; 27:10-19).

Moses, Aaron, and Aaron's sons were to camp on the east side of the tabernacle in front of the Tent of Meeting (3:38). Their position meant that they would march in front of the tabernacle when the tribes were traveling. They were in charge of the rites and sacrifices. No one else could come near the sanctuary (3:38).

The total counted in the census of the Levites was 22,000 (3:39). However, if the numbers of 3:22, 28, 34 are added together, the total is 22,300. The variance has been explained as the loss of one letter in the Hebrew text of 3:28. Thus 8,600 Kohathites should read 8,300 (3:28),[4] making the figure of 22,000 correct. In 3:40-51 it is affirmed that the actual total intended was 22,000.

---

[4] šš is the Hebrew word for six; šlš is Hebrew for three.

5. *Census and redemption of the firstborn males* (3:40–51)

The Lord commanded Moses to take a census of the Israelite firstborn males a month old or more and list them by name (3:40). The purpose of the census was to learn the total number of firstborn of the Israelites in order to substitute Levites for them. The total was found to be 22,273 (3:43), which was 273 more than the number of Levites. As no substitutes were available for the extra 273 Israelites, they had to be redeemed separately by the payment of five shekels of silver (about two ounces) for each one (cf. Lev. 27:6). The standard used was the sanctuary shekel (3:47), the secular shekel being somewhat heavier. The redemption money was to be given to Aaron and his sons (v. 48). The total amount of "silver" ("money," KJV, RSV) weighed 1,365 shekels (3:50), or about thirty-five pounds. Moses gave the redemption money to the priests as the Lord had commanded him (3:51).

D. Census and duties of the Levites (4:1–49)

Chapter 4 gives a more detailed description of the duties of the Kohathites, Gershonites, and Merarites than does the preceding chapter.

1. *Duties of the Kohathites* (4:1–20)

Although Kohath was the second son of Levi and his descendants were listed in that order in chapter 3, the Kohathites are now named first in this census. The change may have occurred because they enjoyed the distinction of having Moses and Aaron as their kinsmen. They may have been listed here according to the clockwise order in which they were encamped around the tabernacle (south, west, north). However, it is also possible that the families are listed here according to the importance or sacredness of their duties rather than by the age of their ancestors.

The previous census had been taken of all males one month old or more (3:39). The second census was limited to men from thirty to fifty who were able to serve in the Tent of Meeting (4:3). Careful instructions were given to Aaron and his sons for dismantling the tabernacle when it was to be moved. First, they were to take down the veil that screened the Holy of Holies and cover the ark with it (4:5). Over that they were to place a covering of "hides of sea cows" ("badgers' skins," KJV; "goatskin," RSV; "porpoise-hide," NEB; "tahash skin," NAB; "fine leather," JB) and over that a cloth of "solid blue" ("violet,"

NEB). Finally, the poles for transport were to be put in place (4:6; cf. Exod. 25:13–15).

The priests were instructed to place a "blue cloth" ("violet," NEB) over "the table of the Presence" ("table of shewbread," KJV). Then they were to place on the cloth the various utensils and the bread, which was not removed while traveling (4:7). Finally, they were to cover all with a scarlet cloth. It, in turn, was to be covered with hides of sea cows (cf. v. 6). Then the poles were to be put in place for transport (v. 8).

Similar instructions were given for covering and transporting the gold lampstand (4:9–10; cf. Exod. 25:31–40), the gold altar of incense (4:11; cf. Exod. 30:1–10), the articles used for ministering in the sanctuary (4:12), and the bronze altar of burnt offering with its utensils (4:13–14; cf. Exod. 27:1–8).

When all the holy articles had been properly covered and the camp was ready to move, the Kohathites would carry them by means of poles or carrying frames. However, they could not touch the holy articles lest they die (4:15; cf. 2 Sam. 6:6–7). Only the priests could handle the sacred objects. Eleazar was put in charge of the tabernacle and everything connected with it. Though the Kohathites carried the articles, Eleazar was personally responsible for them (4:16). The Lord gave a final admonition to Moses and Aaron that the Kohathites should be carefully supervised as they did their work. This precaution was necessary so that they would not die as a result of carelessly handling the sacred articles and thus be cut off from the Levites (vv. 17–19). They could not go in to look at the holy things, even for a moment (literally, "like a swallow," i.e., in the time it would take to gulp), or they would die (v. 20).

2. Duties of the Gershonites (4:21–28)

The second census of the Gershonites was limited to men thirty to fifty who were able to serve in the Tent of Meeting (4:22–23). They were charged with the responsibility for carrying the curtains of the tabernacle, the Tent of Meeting, and the other curtains and coverings associated with them, as well as all equipment used in the service of the tabernacle (vv. 24–26). They were responsible for furnishings less holy than the furnishings entrusted to the Kohathites. All their work was to be done under the direction of Aaron and his sons, particularly Ithamar (vv. 27–28). In 7:7 it is added that they had carts for the purpose of transporting the articles entrusted to them.

3. *Duties of the Merarites* (4:29–33)

The second census of the Merarites was limited to men thirty to fifty who were able to serve in the Tent of Meeting (4:30). Various articles associated with the framework of the tabernacle were assigned to each individual Merarite for carrying (vv. 31–32). It is added in 7:8 that carts were provided for them as for the Gershonites. All their work was to be done under the supervision of Ithamar (4:33).

4. *The numbering of the Levites* (4:34–49)

Moses, Aaron, and other leaders of the community carried out the census of the Levites thirty to fifty years of age as instructed (4:34). The total number of men of the clan of Kohath fit for service in the Tent of Meeting was 2,750 (vv. 35–36). The Gershonites numbered 2,630 (vv. 39–40), and the Merarites numbered 3,200 (vv. 43–44). Altogether, there were 8,580 of the 22,000 Levites previously counted who were eligible for doing the work of serving and carrying the Tent of Meeting and its furnishings (vv. 47–48). Each man was assigned his work and told what to carry (v. 49).

For Further Study

1. In a Bible dictionary or encyclopedia (see bibliography) read articles on priests, Levites, tabernacle, and Tent of Meeting.

2. What purpose(s) did the census of chapter 1 serve other than to determine the military strength of Israel?

3. What is the significance of the Levites not being counted with the other Israelites?

4. Based on the descriptions given in chapters 1–4, draw diagrams of the positions of the Israelite tribes while encamped and while traveling.

Chapter 2

Duties and Regulations
(Numbers 5:1–10:10)

The first four chapters of Numbers are mainly concerned with a census of the Israelites and the duties of the Levites. The chapters that follow (5:1–10:10), by contrast, deal with a number of regulations on a variety of matters without any obvious arrangement or underlying unity. The Israelites were still encamped at Mount Sinai. It was an opportune time for God to give them additional instructions and regulations before they resumed their journey to Canaan.

A. Various regulations governing people and priests (5:1–6:27)

1. *Separation of unclean persons from the camp* (5:1–4)

Because the presence of God dwelled in the tabernacle, the encampment around it was considered holy ground. Therefore, ritually unclean people could not remain in its precincts. Orders were given to remove anyone who had an "infectious skin disease" (5:2; "every leper," KJV, RSV, but the word has a broader meaning; cf. Lev. 13). Also anyone with a discharge of any kind was to be removed (cf. Lev. 15) or one who was ceremonially unclean because of contact with a corpse (see Lev. 19).[1] The regulations may seem somewhat harsh, but uncleanness could not be tolerated because of the Lord's presence in the camp.

---

[1] In God's sight everything was divided into clean and unclean, holy and profane, blessed and cursed. Because uncleanness was considered to be contagious and offensive to God, provisions had to be made to protect the holiness of God from profanation of any kind. Nothing that was unclean could participate in the Hebrew rituals. It either had to be removed or purified through authorized procedures. The most extensive regulations concerning cleanness and uncleanness are found in Leviticus 11–16. For a historical study of cleanness and uncleanness see L. E. Toombs, "Clean and Unclean," in *Interpreter's Dictionary of the Bible*, 5 vols., ed. George Arthur Buttrick et al. (New York/Nashville: Abingdon Press, 1962), 1:641–48.

2. Restitution for wrongs committed (5:5–10)

The regulations of Leviticus 6:1–7 are supplemented in these verses by instructions concerning an original owner or person wronged who had died and left no kinsman to whom restitution could be made. In such cases, first of all, confession was to be made (cf. Lev. 5:5; 16:21). In the absence of a kinsman the amount to be restored would belong to the Lord. Repayment of the amount due Him would be made to the priest (5:7–8). The regulation was based on the important principle that a sin against another person is a sin against God (cf. Ps. 51:4). These sacred "contributions" ("offering," KJV; from a word, "to lift," denoting that which is separated for contribution to sacred purposes) belonged to the priest (5:9–10).

3. The test for unfaithfulness (5:11–31)

The law already provided that the death penalty should be inflicted on both partners guilty of adultery (Lev. 20:10). That law was now supplemented by regulations whereby a suspicious husband, in the absence of witnesses or other proofs, could determine if his wife had been unfaithful to him (5:12–14). The procedure to be followed has often been called the "ordeal of jealousy." It was a humiliating public test inflicted on a wife whose husband was overcome by feelings of suspicion and jealousy (cf. 11:29 for comments on "jealousy").

In such cases the husband took his wife to the priest, together with a grain offering. The usual oil and incense were omitted, for they were symbols of joy and festivity that for this occasion would not be appropriate (5:15; cf. Lev. 2:1). The priest made the woman stand "before the LORD" (5:16), that is, probably before the altar of burnt offering. He then put some "holy water" in a clay jar (v. 17; the term "holy water" is not found elsewhere in the Old Testament; it was probably running water that had been sanctified). Then the priest put some dust from the tabernacle floor in the water (perhaps related symbolically to Gen. 3:14). He loosened the woman's hair (as a sign of mourning and shame) and placed her husband's grain offering in her hands while he held the jar of bitter water (5:18). Then he put the woman under oath. He instructed her that if she had not been unfaithful to her husband, no harm would come to her. However, if she were guilty of unfaithfulness, her thigh would waste away and her abdomen would swell when she drank the bitter water (5:19–22; cf. the cup of wrath, Jer. 25:15–29).

The exact nature of the affliction is uncertain. Some have assumed that a woman who had become pregnant by an immoral act would be punished by having a miscarriage.

The passage states further that the priest was to write on a scroll the curse he had invoked and then wash the ink into the bitter water. Symbolically the curse was conveyed to the potion itself (cf. Ezek. 2:9–3:3). The woman was required to drink the water (5:23–24), having previously given the grain offering to the priest, who burned a handful of it on the altar after waving it before the Lord (vv. 25–26). A literal reading of these verses would make it appear that the woman drank the water two times, once before and once after the grain was burned. If the woman was guilty of unfaithfulness, the curse would bring bitter physical suffering on her and she would become accursed among her people (v. 27). If innocent, she would suffer no harmful effects from the potion (v. 28).

The narrative closes with a statement that the husband would be guiltless, even if his suspicions were unfounded (5:31). In either case the woman suffered. If guilty, she suffered a bodily affliction. If innocent, she was humiliated and degraded in public by her husband's unfounded suspicions. It should also be noted that there was no provision for requiring a husband to submit to a similar ordeal if his wife suspected him of unfaithfulness.

4. Law of the Nazirite (6:1–21)

The law of the "Nazirite"[2] (incorrectly spelled "Nazarite," KJV) provided an opportunity for a man or woman to assume a "special vow" (literally, "to vow a vow") of total separation to the Lord for a fixed period of time. The vow was not for a lifetime, though it is generally supposed that Samson (Judg. 13:5) and Samuel (1 Sam. 1:11) were under a lifetime commitment to the Nazirite vow.

The person who assumed the Nazirite vow took three obligations on himself: (1) He was not to consume the grape in any form, not the wine or even the seeds or skin (6:3–4; cf. the vow of the Recabites, Jer. 35:1–6). (2) He was not to cut his hair (6:5). Hair was a symbol of strength and power, and its free growth showed that the person's strength was dedicated to God. (3) He was not to touch a corpse, even

---

[2]The word comes from a Hebrew word that means "to separate/consecrate." It should not be confused with Nazareth/Nazarene, which is spelled differently in Hebrew and comes from a word that means either "watchtower" or "sprout."

of a close relative (vv. 6–8). The latter restriction prevented a person from participating in the filial custom of preparing bodies of loved ones for burial.

The symbolic meaning of these restrictions can only be guessed. Perhaps the first symbolized separation from pleasure; the second, separation from vain self-preoccupation; and the third, separation from family life. By his actions the Nazirite was a constant reminder to his community of what total separation to God should mean. In Amos's time the consciences of the faithless Israelites were so troubled by the Nazirites in their midst that they forced them to drink wine and thus break their vow (Amos 2:11–12).

A Nazirite's dedicated hair was considered defiled if he was present when someone died suddenly. Upon being pronounced clean seven days later, he was required to shave his hair on that same day (6:9). Then the next day he was to bring two doves or pigeons to the priest, who would offer one as a sin offering and the other as a burnt offering (vv. 10–11). He was required to bring a year-old male lamb as a guilt offering and then to begin the entire period of his vow all over again (v. 12).

When the period of separation was completed, the Nazirite was required to bring specified offerings to the priest at the entrance of the Tent of Meeting (6:13–17). There he shaved off his hair and burned it in the fire that was under the sacrifice of the fellowship offering (6:18; perhaps Acts 18:18 and 21:26 refer to Paul's completion of a Nazirite vow). The priest took part of the offerings brought by the Nazirite and waved them before the Lord. After the vow was completed, the Nazirite could once again drink wine (6:19–20; cf. Deut. 23:21–23, which warns of the importance of keeping vows).

5. The priestly blessing (6:22–27)

This blessing, frequently heard today, is perhaps the best known benediction in the Old Testament. It does not appear to be connected with what precedes or follows. Aaron and his sons were instructed to bless the people. "The LORD make his face to shine upon you" means to look with pleasure or favor, i.e., to be friendly. "The LORD turn his face toward you" suggests recognition and approval. To "give you peace" meant more than absence of war or discord to the ancient Hebrew. "Peace" connoted wholeness and well-being in every way. By putting His name on the people of Israel (6:27; cf. the slave who was branded with his owner's name), Aaron and his sons would convey that the Israelites belonged to the Lord and were thus assured of blessing.

B. Regulations concerning the offerings of the leaders (7:1–89)

This chapter, one of the longest in the Bible, tells about offerings the leaders ("princes," KJV, NAB; "chief men," NEB) brought generously and on their own initiative (cf. the generous giving of 1 Chron. 29). It employs the repetitious style of language that has already been encountered in Numbers. This characteristic style was probably used for emphasis and solemnity.

1. *Offerings of the leaders* (7:1–11)

The same day the tabernacle was finished and consecrated (7:1; cf. Exod. 40), the leaders who had assisted Moses in the census (1:4) brought offerings (7:2). The gifts they brought were an ox from each leader and a cart from every two (v. 3). The Lord instructed Moses to accept the gifts and to give them to the Levites to be used in the work at the Tent of Meeting (vv. 4–5). Moses divided the offerings among the Gershonites and Merarites according to the requirements of their work (vv. 7–8). He did not share the offerings with the Kohathites because they were required to carry on their shoulders the "holy things" ("service of the sanctuary," KJV) for which they were responsible (7:9; but cf. 2 Sam. 6:3).

On the day the altar was anointed (cf. Exod. 40:10), the leaders began bringing their offerings for its dedication. On successive days each leader brought his offering (7:10–11).

2. *Daily offerings for the dedication of the altar* (7:12–83)

The rest of the chapter is almost wholly devoted to a listing of offerings brought by each leader and employs an almost identically repeated formula. The leaders are not listed in the same order as in chapter 1 (cf. 1:5–15), but are listed according to the order of the tribes in the camp (cf. 2:3–31). The gifts of each leader were identical. They consisted of materials for four of the principal offerings: the burnt, grain, fellowship, and sin offerings (cf. Lev. 1:1–5:13). Each one, beginning with Nahshon, brought a silver plate weighing 130 shekels (about 3¼ pounds) and a silver sprinkling bowl weighing seventy shekels (about 1¾ pounds). Each was filled with fine flour mixed with oil as a grain offering (7:13). Each leader also brought a gold ladle weighing ten shekels (about four ounces) filled with incense (v. 14). Each one also brought various animals, twenty-one in number, to be sacrificed as a "fellowship offering" ("peace offering," KJV, RSV).

3. Summary of the offerings (7:84–88)

After the listing of the offerings of each leader, the totals were then given of all their offerings. The total offerings were extremely large and reveal the generosity of the leaders. Such wealth of former slaves has been questioned but can be explained in the light of Exodus 12:32, 35–36.

4. The voice of the Lord (7:89)

This verse is not specifically related to what has preceded. It is a fulfillment of the promise of Exodus 25:22. As promised there, Moses heard God speaking to him from between the two cherubim above the "atonement cover" ("mercy seat," KJV, RSV, NASB) of the ark of the testimony. The fact that no specific speech follows the verse has led some scholars to conclude that the speech was either lost or displaced. However, it is more likely that the verse was intended as a general statement and not as an introduction to a divine oracle.

C. Additional laws and regulations (8:1–10:10)

1. The gold lampstand (8:1–4)

Aaron was given the responsibility of setting up the lamps to provide light for the area in front of the gold lampstand (8:2; called the Menorah in Judaism today; cf. Exod. 25:31–40; Zech. 4:1–6, 10–14). There were seven lamps (seven frequently symbolizes completeness in the Old Testament). Each lamp consisted of a small bowl of oil with a wick. A lamp was attached to the top of the lampstand's central stem, and also each of the three branches on either side of the stem had its lamps. The lampstand was placed against the south curtain of the Holy Place of the tabernacle. As the only source of light in the Holy Place, it cast its light toward the north side, where the table of the bread of the Presence was located. It is uncertain whether the flame burned continuously or only at night (cf. Exod. 25:37; 27:21; 30:8; Lev. 24:1–4; 2 Chron. 13:11).

A brief description of the lampstand is given. It was made of hammered gold, i.e., fashioned from one solid plate of gold, not of separate pieces joined together. It was ornamented with gold flowers and was made according to a pattern that Lord had revealed to Moses (8:4; cf. Exod. 25:9, 31, 40; 37:17–24).

2. *The Levites* (8:5–26)

These verses describe the Levites as an offering brought to the Lord by Israel at the Lord's command (cf. the ordination ceremony of the priests in Lev. 8). The words were addressed to Moses, who officiated at the setting apart of the Levites, as he had done for the priests (cf. 3:5–13).

a) *Their purification and dedication* (8:5–22)

Moses was instructed by the Lord to separate the Levites from the other Israelites and make them ceremonially clean (8:6). To accomplish this cleansing, he was to sprinkle "water of cleansing" on them ("water of purifying," KJV; "water of expiation," RSV; literally, "water of sin"). Then their bodies were to be shaved (a practice also followed by Egyptian priests), and their clothes were to be washed (8:7; cf. Exod. 29:8; Lev. 8:7–13, where priests were given new garments). They were to bring two young bulls for offerings (8:8). In front of the Tent of Meeting the assembled Israelite community would lay hands on the Levites as an act of identification (vv. 9–10). Then Aaron was to present the Levites before the Lord as a wave offering from the people (v. 11). The waving here was symbolic, representing the waving of 22,000 Levite men before the altar (cf. 3:39). After this, they would be ready for the Lord's service.

As a part of the ritual just described, the Levites were to lay their hands on the heads of the bulls brought for a sin offering and for a burnt offering (8:12; cf. 6:11; Lev. 1:4; 4:4). By means of the ceremony the Levites were set apart from the rest of the Israelites as a possession of God (8:14).

Upon the completion of the purification ritual, the Levites were ready to begin their work (8:15). Again we are told that they had been taken by God in place of the firstborn males of the Israelites (8:16–18; cf. 3:11–13). The Lord gave them as "gifts" (literally, "given ones") to Aaron and his sons (8:19). Their purpose was twofold: (1) to do the work at the Tent of Meeting on behalf of the Israelites and (2) to make atonement for the people so that no plague would afflict them when they approached the sanctuary (8:19). By dwelling around the tent, the Levites protected the people from unauthorized contact with God that could have disastrous results for all the people. In a final summary statement we are told that all the Lord's commands concerning the Levites were carefully carried out (8:20–22).

b) *Their age for service* (8:23–26)

In 4:3 the age limits for Levitical service were given as thirty to fifty. Here they are twenty-five to fifty (8:24–25; cf. 1 Chron. 23:24, where the lower age limit was twenty with no stated upper limit). After retirement a Levite could still assist the other Levites but could not do the actual work (8:25–26).

3. *Regulations for an additional Passover* (9:1–14)

Chronologically the events described in this chapter preceded the census of chapter 1 (9:1; cf. 1:1). The people had been encamped at Sinai for almost a year, and Passover time was again approaching. The Lord reminded Moses that the people should observe the Passover at the appointed time, the evening (literally, "between the two evenings") of the fourteenth day of the first month (9:2–3). The people celebrated Passover in the manner commanded by the Lord (9:4–5; cf. Exod. 12:1–20, 43–49).

Some of the people were ceremonially unclean and were therefore unable to keep the Passover at the appointed time. The reason was that they had had contact with a corpse (9:6; cf. Lev. 7:21; 22:1–8; Num. 19:11; 1 Sam. 21:4–6). They came to Moses and asked why they should be kept from observing the Passover with their fellow Israelites (9:7). Their question probably does not imply that they were unaware of the regulations but rather that they were asking for a modification of the rules.

To his credit Moses did not voice his opinion but said, "Wait" (literally, "stand"; "stand still," KJV). He wanted to consult the Lord before he answered (9:8; cf. 15:34; 27:5; Exod. 25:22; Lev. 24:10–23 for other examples of seeking divine direction). The Lord answered by granting two exceptions for keeping the Passover at the stated time: (1) uncleanness because of contact with a corpse, and (2) a journey that prevented one's participation (9:10). Those who were in either of these categories were allowed to celebrate the Passover exactly one month later (9:11; cf. 2 Chron. 30:1–27). The second Passover was to be observed in precisely the same manner as the first (9:11–12).

Apart from these exceptions, anyone who failed to observe the first Passover each year would be cut off from his people (9:13). The phrase "cut off from his people" is found frequently in the Old Testament (e.g., Gen. 17:14; Lev. 7:20–21). It is uncertain whether the threat meant a death penalty for the offender or excommunication from the community. If we assume that the death penalty was intended, then it is unclear whether the execution of it was by divine or human agency.

The "alien" ("stranger," KJV, JB; "foreigner," TEV) was also allowed to participate in the Passover if he observed all its rules and regulations. The same regulations applied to the resident alien as to the native-born Israelite (9:14; cf. Exod. 12:45, 48–49; Deut. 10:18–19).

4. The fiery cloud over the tabernacle (9:15–23)

Once again the narrative reverts to an event that preceded the census. It refers to the day of the erection of the tabernacle, called here "the Tent of the Testimony" (9:15; cf. Exod. 40:34–38). On the day the tabernacle was completed, a cloud covered it; at night the cloud looked like fire. From that day on, whenever the cloud lifted from over the tent, the Israelites set out on their journey. Wherever the cloud settled, the Israelites stopped and made camp (9:17–18). The cloud sometimes remained stationary for only a night, or it remained unmoved for as much as a year. The Israelites were careful to travel only when the cloud moved and to remain encamped when the cloud rested over the tabernacle (vv. 19–23). Whether moving or stationary, the cloud was a visible reminder of God's guiding presence among His people. The Israelites were being taught to follow God's guidance.

5. The two silver trumpets (10:1–10)

The time was approaching for Israel to leave Sinai and journey toward Canaan. While traveling, it was essential to have some means of instant communication for assembling the people and for beginning the day's march. Therefore, the Lord instructed Moses to make two trumpets of silver, each to be hammered out of a single plate of silver (10:2). The sounding of both trumpets was a signal for all the people to assemble before Moses at the Tent of Meeting (v. 3). If one trumpet was sounded, only the leaders were to assemble before Moses (10:4; cf. 1:16).

A different kind of "trumpet blast" (10:5; "blow an alarm," KJV, RSV) would serve as a signal for the tribes to set out on the march. The difference in sound between the two signals in 10:4–5 cannot be known. The first blast was to signal the tribes on the east side to set out. At the second blast the tribes on the south were to set out, and only the priests could blow the trumpets. This regulation was fixed for the present and for all future generations (v. 8).

Occasions for blowing the trumpets after Israel's arrival in Canaan were also specified. They were to be blown when the people went into battle against an oppressing enemy in their own land. God would remember His people on those occasions and rescue them from their foes (10:9; cf. Ps. 44:22–24; 2 Chron. 13:12–18). The other occasion for blowing the trumpets was at times of rejoicing, specifically at the appointed feasts and "New Moon festivals" (10:10; "beginnings of your months," KJV, RSV). On those occasions they were to sound the trumpets over the burnt offerings and "fellowship offerings" ("peace offerings," KJV, RSV, NASB; "shared offerings," NEB). By so doing, the people would be brought to the remembrance of God.

For Further Study

1. In a Bible dictionary or encyclopedia (see bibliography) read articles on leprosy, clean and unclean, women in the Old Testament, Nazirite, and Passover.

2. What do you believe were the purposes of the three-fold restrictions placed on a person who assumed the Nazirite vow?

3. Make a study of the treatment of foreigners in various cultures of the ancient Near East.

PART TWO: *The Journey From Sinai to Moab*

Chapter 3

The Journey From Sinai to the Desert of Paran
(Numbers 10:11–12:16)

It was more than a year since the Israelites' departure from Egypt. By this time the painful memories of oppression in that land must have been gradually fading from their thoughts. Now their minds were occupied with plans for settling in the Promised Land to which God was leading them. Bolstered by the recently made covenant at Sinai and by the visible reminders of God's presence with them, they faced the future with confidence. Within a few weeks they expected to be settling down in Canaan. They did not anticipate that a destination which seemed to be within their grasp would take almost forty years to reach.

A. The departure from Sinai (10:11–36)

Israel had been encamped at Mount Sinai for almost a year. The period of preparation and instruction was complete, and the time had now come to possess the land.

1. *The time of departure* (10:11–12)

On the twentieth day of the second month of the second year after Israel left Egypt, the cloud above the tabernacle lifted (10:11). It was the signal to break camp and begin the journey. It was only nineteen days after the census had been taken (cf. 1:1) and eleven months and twenty days since their arrival at Sinai. Obediently they set out and traveled from place to place until the cloud came to "rest" (from a word meaning "to dwell") in the Desert of Paran (10:12). The exact location of Paran is uncertain, but it was probably in the north central part of the Sinai Peninsula.

2. The order of the march (10:13–28)

Following the instructions already given them (cf. 2:1–9), the tribe of Judah, under Nahshon, the son of Amminadab, set out at the head of the march accompanied by the tribes of Issachar and Zebulun (10:14–16). They were followed by the other tribes in the order already given by the Lord (cf. 2:10–31). After Judah set out, the tabernacle was taken down and packed for travel according to previously given instructions (cf. chaps. 3–4). The Gershonites and Merarites loaded the tabernacle and its furnishings on wagons and set out behind Judah (10:17). The order of march given here is somewhat different from that described in 2:17 (cf. comments there).

The Gershonites and Merarites were followed by the tribes encamped on the south side: Reuben, Simeon, and Gad (10:18–20; cf. spelling "Deuel" in 10:20 and 1:14, with "Reuel" in most MT manuscripts at 2:14, NIV margin). Behind them came the Kohathites, carrying the holy articles. The order of march described in these verses allowed time for the tabernacle to be erected at each campsite to await the sacred objects borne by the Kohathites (10:21).

The tribes who encamped on the south side were followed by those who encamped on the west side: Ephraim, Manasseh, and Benjamin (10:22–24). Bringing up the rear were the tribes who camped on the north side: Dan, Asher, and Naphtali (vv. 25–27). This order of march was preserved whenever the Israelites traveled from place to place (v. 28).

3. Moses' invitation to Hobab (10:29–32)

Moses invited Hobab to continue the journey with the Israelites to Canaan with a promise to "treat you well" (10:29; "do you good," RSV; "deal generously with you," NEB). The words are usually interpreted as a promise to share in the spoils of conquest, not in the division of the land itself. If so, it can be understood why he preferred to return to his own land and kindred. Moses appealed to Hobab to remain with them to serve as a guide ("our eyes"). He also acknowledged that Hobab's familiarity with the land would enable him to know the good camping places (v. 31). This statement seems to conflict with the promise of divine guidance and may reveal a lapse of Moses' confidence in God. It may also serve as a reminder that divine guidance should be associated with the exercise of reason and human effort. Hobab's answer to the appeal is not given, but Judges 1:16 and 4:11 seem to imply that Moses prevailed over Hobab.

The name of Moses' father-in-law varies in the Old Testament. He is called Jethro (Exod. 3:1; 18:1) and also Jether (4:18; here English translations change Jether to "Jethro" to conform with other occurrences of this name). Then too he is called Reuel (2:18) and Hobab (Judg. 4:11). Here in Numbers 10:29 Hobab is not Moses' father-in-law but is called the son of Reuel ("Raguel," KJV, though the Hebrew word is the same as "Reuel" in Exod. 2:18, KJV). Various attempts have been made to harmonize the spellings. The documentary hypothesis sees different literary sources behind the names. Some argue that people frequently had more than one name in the ancient Near East (e.g., Azariah, 2 Kings 15:1; Uzziah, 2 Kings 15:13). Others use the rendering "brother-in-law" (NIV margin: "father-in-law") in Judges 4:11 to conform to the relationship indicated in Numbers 10:29.

Another problem involved in the identity of Moses' father-in-law is that sometimes he is called a Midianite (10:29; Exod. 2:16) and sometimes a Kenite (Judg. 1:16; 4:11). This question is more easily resolved than the first, as scholars are generally agreed that the Kenites were a nomadic tribe that was probably a branch of the Midianites.

4. *Moses' prayer* (10:33–36)

After leaving Sinai (called "the mountain of the LORD" only here in the Old Testament; the expression is sometimes used of Jerusalem, e.g., Isa. 2:3; cf. Ps. 24:3), the Israelites traveled three days before finding a place to camp. Ordinarily the ark followed the tribes that encamped on the east side of the tabernacle (cf. 10:14–17), but on this occasion the ark was carried in front to seek a resting place for the people (10:33, cf. Deut. 1:33).

Whenever the ark set out with the cloud over the people as the journey began (called "the cloud of the LORD" only in 10:34 and Exod. 40:38), Moses offered a prayer. The prayer seems more appropriate as a battle cry (10:35; cf. Ps. 68:1), but perhaps it suggests that Israel in march was God's army. When the ark came to rest, Moses offered another prayer (10:36), which seems to suggest the safe return of the ark to its sanctuary after a victory over an enemy.

B. Complaints of the people (11:1–12:16)

The complaining spirit of the Israelites characterized them almost from the moment they left Egypt (cf. Exod. 14:11–12). It revealed a singular lack of faith in God's ability to take care of them. They had resumed their travels only a short time before they also renewed their complaints. They had groaned under the oppression of slavery in Egypt, but they found their freedom to be a burden, also.

1. *The complaint at Taberah* (11:1-3)

The people complained about their hardships; no specific problem is described. On similar occasions earlier God had dealt gently with them, but now His anger was aroused (11:1; literally, "his nose became hot," a vivid Hebrew idiom found about eighty times in the Old Testament). He sent a fire that burned among them and consumed some outlying parts of the camp (11:1). The people cried out in anguish to Moses, who in turn prayed to the Lord (perhaps they should have done the same thing!). It was not the only time that Moses interceded on behalf of his people (e.g., Exod. 32:32). The fire was quenched, thanks to Moses' intercession. The place was given the name Taberah, which means "burning" (11:3). Its exact location is unknown.

2. *The complaints at Kibroth Hattaavah* (11:4-35)

a) *Complaint about the manna* (11:4-9)

God's angry warning did not silence the rebellious people for long. Incited by the "rabble" ("mixed multitude," KJV; cf. Exod. 12:38, though the Hebrew phrase there is different) who followed them out of Egypt and who began to crave food other than manna, the Israelites began wailing for meat to eat (11:4). Though they had flocks, these would have been insufficient for a daily supply of meat (cf. vv. 21-22).

As on an earlier occasion (cf. Exod. 16:3), the people began to idealize life in Egypt. They recalled the fish they had eaten in Egypt "at no cost" (11:5; "freely," KJV; "for nothing," RSV; "for the asking," NEB). It is true that fish was available in great quantities in Egypt and inexpensive, but as slaves the Israelites probably did not enjoy food in abundance. When recalling the past, memory usually filters out the harsh, painful experiences and remembers only the pleasant things.

The Israelites' craving was not just for meat but also for the strong flavor of cucumbers, melons, leeks, onions, and garlic (11:5; the Greek historian Herodotus recorded that the pyramid workers ate radishes, onions, and leeks). By retrospect Egypt's garlic was preferable to the daily provision of manna (cf. Exod. 16:1-21). They had lost their appetite for it (11:6; "our soul is dried away," KJV; "our strength is dried up," RSV; "our throats are parched," NEB). The sight of manna made them sick!

Verses 7–9 describe the appearance of manna and ways of preparing it. In size it was like the seed of the coriander plant, no larger than a small pea. It looked like "resin" ("bdellium," KJV, RSV, JB, a yellow transparent gum; Exod. 16:31 describes manna as white, however). It was ground in a handmill or crushed in a mortar before being cooked or made into cakes. (This description conflicts with many scholars' identification of manna with the secretion of the tamarisk tree, which does not harden sufficiently for grinding.) It tasted as though it had been cooked in olive oil (11:8). It appeared on the ground like dew each morning, except on the Sabbath (11:9; Exod. 16:14, 25).

b) *Moses' complaint to the Lord* (11:10–15)

It was not unusual to hear an Israelite complain. Now, however, the wailing of the people as they sat at the entrance to their tents made Moses begin to grumble. Their wailing made the Lord extremely angry, which displeased Moses (11:10). He asked God why He had brought so much trouble on him. He wanted to know what he had done to displease Him so that the burden of all the Israelites was placed on him (v. 11). Moses seemed to be harboring a lingering trace of resentment that when God originally had called him as a deliverer, He had done so against his will (cf. Exod. 3:1–4:17).

Petulantly, Moses complained that his lot was that of a mother with her infant or a "nurse" ("foster father," NAB; a masculine word in Hebrew) with a crying baby (11:12). Also, it was too much to ask him to provide meat for such a great multitude (11:13; cf. Mark 8:4). Overcome by a spirit of self-pity, Moses said he could not carry such a burden alone (11:14). In his anguish he forgot God's promise: "My Presence will go with you, and I will give you rest" (Exod. 33:14). In despair he asked to be killed immediately if he had found favor in God's eyes (11:15; for similar requests for death cf. Exod. 32:32; 1 Kings 19:4; Job 3; Jer. 15:10; 20:14–18; Jonah 4:3). He did not want to live to see the failure of all his hopes and efforts on behalf of Israel. Once he had been willing to die for his people (Exod. 32:32), but now he only wanted to die.

c) *The Lord's response to Moses* (11:16–23)

God recognized the legitimacy of Moses' anguish. The burden really was too much for one person. Therefore, He did not rebuke him. Instead, He instructed him to bring seventy "elders" (from a word, "to have a beard," "to be old") to the Tent of Meeting, men who were proven leaders and officials among the people (11:16). Moses had cried for divine help, and God gave him human help. He promised to take some of the Spirit that was on Moses and put the Spirit on the elders so that they could share in carrying the burdens of the people (v. 17). They would in effect share the Complaints Department with Moses!

The Lord told Moses to instruct the people to make themselves ceremonially clean for the next day when meat would be provided (11:18). Angrily He promised to give them meat—not just for one day but for an entire month (literally, "a month of days"). They would become so stuffed on the meat that it would come out of their nostrils, and the sight of it would nauseate them (vv. 19–20). God was going to punish them severely for complaining that they had left Egypt (v. 20). Their attitude revealed that they had rejected the Lord and had no confidence in His power to take care of them.

Even Moses was incredulous that so much meat could be provided for so many people. He protested that slaughtering all their flocks and herds would not provide sufficient meat. Catching all the fish in the sea would not be sufficient for such a hungry horde (11:21–22). The Lord challenged Moses' unbelief: "Is the LORD's arm too short?" (v. 23; i.e., Is He too weak or powerless to accomplish what He promised? Cf. Isa. 50:2; 59:1).

d) *The Spirit on the elders* (11:24–25)

Moses related to the people what the Lord had told him. He brought seventy of their elders before the tent (11:24; the method of their selection is not stated). The Lord came down in a cloud and took of the Spirit that rested on Moses and placed the Spirit on the elders. They began to prophesy (11:25; "they fell into a prophetic ecstasy," NEB; "they began to shout like prophets," TEV). Their unusual behavior was a sign of endowment with the Spirit. (For other examples of unusual prophetic behavior, cf. 1 Sam. 10:10; 18:10; 19:23–24; 2 Kings 2:15; Isa. 11:2.) As their normal function was that of administration, not prophesying, this manifestation of the Spirit did not continue. "They did not do so again" (literally, "and not they added"; KJV translates as "and did not cease" as does the Latin Vulgate).

e) *The Spirit on Eldad and Medad* (11:26–30)

Two men named Eldad and Medad, otherwise unmentioned in the Bible, remained in the camp. They were "listed among the elders" ("enrolled with the seventy," NEB; literally, "they were among the written"), but did not join the seventy at the tent (11:26). Perhaps only seventy of a larger number of elders were chosen. Yet the Spirit came on them, and they prophesied, just as the others had. A young man, seeing them, ran and reported to Moses what they were doing. Joshua, who already had served Moses (cf. Exod. 17:9; 33:11), immediately suggested that Moses stop them (11:28; literally, "restrain them"; cf. John's protest, Mark 9:38–41). Perhaps he was afraid that Moses' honor and authority would be diminished by men who had not received the Spirit from him.

Moses demonstrated his nobility and lack of personal ambition by gently rebuking Joshua. "Are you jealous for my sake?" ("jealous" is from a word meaning color produced in the face by deep emotion; hence, to get excited, worked up). He would be happy if all the Lord's people were prophets and all possessed the Spirit (11:29). Moses had no desire to control the work of the Spirit among his people, for he had their welfare, rather than his own preeminence, uppermost.

f) *The feast of quails* (11:31–35)

The narrative, interrupted by the selection of the seventy elders, now resumes with the fulfillment of the promise of abundant meat for the people. The Lord sent a wind that drove quails in from the sea (understood by some as the Gulf of Aqabah and by others as the Mediterranean Sea). They flew not more than three feet above the ground (some translations understand that the birds covered the ground to a depth of three feet). They were so numerous that they were spread out as far as a person could walk in two days, and they were very easy to catch in great numbers (11:31). Observers have noted that quails still migrate from Africa to Europe in great numbers in the spring and return in the fall. Flocks of quails regularly appear on the Mediterranean coast of the Sinai Peninsula in the spring and fall and are easy to catch.

The Israelites gathered great quantities of the quails. No one took less than ten homers (estimated as forty to sixty bushels). They spread many of the birds on the ground to cure by drying and began to feast on others (11:32). Even while the meat was still unchewed in their mouths, the Lord struck them in anger with a plague, killing many of them (11:33; cf. 16:49; 25:9; Exod. 15:26; 32:35). The place was named Kibroth Hattaavah (i.e., graves of craving/eager desire), for there they buried the people who had craved the meat (11:34). Kibroth Hattaavah has been tentatively identified with Ruweis el-Eberig, a few miles northeast of Mount Sinai. From that place the people traveled to Hazeroth (perhaps modern Ain Khudra) and remained there (v. 35).

3. *The complaint of Miriam and Aaron* (12:1–16)

The people of Israel had complained on numerous occasions. Moses had complained once about the burden placed on him. The present narrative describes a complaint that Aaron and Miriam, Moses' brother and sister, directed against him. These two had shared the responsibilities of leadership with Moses (cf. Mic. 6:4). Aaron was the high priest, and Miriam was a prophetess (Exod. 15:20; 28:3).

They began criticizing Moses because of his marriage to a Cushite woman (12:1). The only marriage of Moses that is known was his marriage to Zipporah (Exod. 2:16–22; 4:25; 18:2), but she was called a Midianite (Exod. 2:16) or Kenite (Judg. 1:16; 4:11).

A number of explanations of the term "Cushite" used in 12:1 have been proposed by scholars: (1) Most commonly, Cush (a slightly different spelling in Hebrew from Cushite) is another name for Ethiopia; if so, Moses married again; there is some evidence that Moses did not get along with Zipporah (Exod. 18:2); the tradition that Moses married an Ethiopian is quite ancient. (2) It refers to the Cassites, a people who lived east of Babylonia; if so, the woman was another wife. (3) The Kusi were people of northern Arabia; if this identification is correct, the woman could be Zipporah or someone else. (4) Habakkuk 3:7 equates Cushan (another spelling for Cush?) with Midian; if Cushan is the same as Cushite, the reference is to Zipporah. (5) By the use of gematria, Cushite means "a woman of beautiful appearance," and is not to be taken as a proper name;[1] if this interpretation is accepted, the woman could be Zipporah.

If the complaint of Miriam and Aaron was about Moses' marriage to a foreigner (whether Zipporah or another), it reflects the antiquity of racial prejudice in every part of the world.

It is not uncommon for family members to dislike the wife of one of their relatives. There may be no more profound basis for the unhappiness of Miriam and Aaron than this. However, 12:2 offers another explanation of their unhappiness with Moses—wounded pride: "Has the LORD spoken only through Moses? Hasn't he also spoken through us?" They did not deny Moses' right to leadership of the people or his prophetic function. They were jealous that they did not receive equal

---

[1]See p. 10 for an explanation of gematria. According to this system the Hebrew letters of "Cushite" in 12:1 add up to 736; the Hebrew letters of "beautiful of appearance" also add up to 736. Therefore, according to the logic of gematria, Cushite means nothing more than "beautiful of appearance."

acclaim and recognition as spokesmen for the Lord.

Parenthetically, we are told that Moses was a humble person (12:3; "meek," KJV; "a most devout creature," MOFFATT), more than anyone else on earth. The Hebrew word does not mean cowardice but "patient, bearing wrongs without resistance." It can in some contexts mean "poor" or "afflicted." The word suggests a person of gentle disposition, modest, and not "pushy." Moses was a person who did not fight for his rights or fight to establish his reputation and status among people. This quality enabled him to keep silent in the face of their complaints. As a man of faith, he believed that God would vindicate him of unjust accusations. Therefore, there was no need to take up his own defense.

The Lord heard the complaints of Miriam and Aaron and immediately came to Moses' defense. The Lord demanded that the three of them appear before Him at the Tent of Meeting (12:4). There He came down in a pillar of cloud and summoned Aaron and Miriam before Him (v. 5). He told them that other prophets of the Lord received their messages indirectly through visions and dreams (v. 6). Moses was faithful in the administration of the affairs of all the people of God "in all my house" (v. 7; cf. Heb. 3:2, 5). As a result he enjoyed the unique privilege of direct and intimate communication with God. God spoke "face to face" (literally, "mouth to mouth") to His "servant" Moses (v. 8; the term "servant" is used regularly in the Old Testament of heroes of the faith, e.g., David).

Moses was so close that "he sees the form of the LORD" (12:8). In light of statements that a person cannot see God and live (Exod. 33:20; Judg. 13:22; Isa. 6:5; however, cf. Gen. 16:13; 32:30; Exod. 33:23; Deut. 4:33; Judg. 6:22–23; Ezek. 1:26–28; John 1:18; 14:9), we should not read too much into this statement. There is a hiddenness about God that is greater than that between two people. One person may say to a friend, "We see each other"; however, they rarely know all about the other person. No one can know all about God, not even a Moses. Yet it would be equally wrong not to acknowledge that Moses had a unique personal encounter with God.

God's anger was great against Aaron and Miriam as He departed (12:9). The moment the cloud lifted, Aaron saw that Miriam was covered with leprosy like snow (v. 10; the Hebrew word translated "leprosy" could indicate a number of skin diseases).

Various explanations have been proposed for Aaron's escape from punishment. Perhaps Miriam took the lead in the complaint and therefore merited the penalty. Perhaps because he was the high priest, Aaron could not be allowed to become unclean and therefore unfit for his priestly duties. Perhaps his prompt repentance on seeing Miriam saved him from a similar fate.

Aaron pleaded with Moses for forgiveness of the foolish sin they had committed. He asked that Miriam not be treated like a stillborn baby whose flesh is already half consumed even as it comes from its mother's womb (12:11–12). People stricken with the terrible disease of leprosy in ancient times were cast out of the community and treated as though they were already dead. Aaron pleaded that his sister not meet such a fate. Like Job's friends, Aaron was required to seek the mediation of the one whose intimacy with God he had questioned (cf. Job 42:7–9).

Once again assuming the role of intercessor, Moses pleaded with God to heal Miriam (12:13). He did not rebuke his sister or exult over her punishment.

The Lord cited the case of a woman whose father had spit in her face to show his contempt for her as justification for Miriam's punishment (12:14; cf. Deut. 25:9; Job 30:10; Isa. 50:6; Matt. 27:30). Such a person was isolated for seven days as punishment. God could do no less to Miriam in the present situation. He ordered that she be confined outside the camp for seven days before she could return (12:14). Her position as a leader did not exempt her from punishment. The law required that all alike, regardless of rank, be excluded from the community in case of leprosy (cf. 2 Kings 15:5; 2 Chron. 26:21).

During Miriam's period of banishment the people remained encamped in Hazeroth. Though not stated, the story implies that she was healed of the disease. Afterward they journeyed to the Desert of Paran and made camp (12:15–16).

Some important lessons from the experience of Miriam and Aaron are the following: (1) People do not always immediately reveal the real reason for their complaints. (2) One who attacks a servant of the Lord risks God's wrath. (3) We may safely leave our defense (or vengeance) in the Lord's hands when we know we are innocent of false charges.

For Further Study

1. In a Bible dictionary or encyclopedia (see bibliography) read articles on manna, Paran, elders, and Cush.

2. Why are people so quick to complain about an unpleasant situation in which they find themselves?

3. Make a study of the Spirit of God in the Old Testament.

4. Recall some times when God vindicated a position you had taken that may have caused misunderstanding or criticism.

5. With the use of commentaries make a study of the identification of the Cushite woman whom Moses married.

Chapter 4

The Wanderings in the Desert—I

(Numbers 13:1–15:41)

Chapters 13–21 contain all that is known about the years spent in the desert (cf. the summary in Deut. 1:6–3:29). The distance from Sinai to Kadesh Barnea was an eleven-days' journey (Deut. 1:2). Now poised on the southern edge of the Promised Land, the Israelites cautiously made their plans for entering it. Though the land was theirs by promise, it was occupied by other peoples; and they would be considered as invaders to be resisted. At Kadesh Barnea they lost heart and were unwilling to push on into the land. Their attitude brought God's wrath on them and postponed their entrance into the land for thirty-eight years (Deut. 2:14).

A. The twelve spies (13:1–33)

1. Appointment of the spies (13:1–16)

Was the appointment of spies a wise precaution or a concession to the people's faithlessness? Deuteronomy 1:19–23 suggests that it was the latter. The text says only that the Lord authorized the mission (13:1–2). Twelve spies were chosen, one leader from each tribe (vv. 4–15). They were not the same men who were named as leaders in 1:5–15. Except for Caleb and Joshua, the other men are not mentioned again. In 13:16 we learn that Moses changed the name of Hoshea son of Nun to Joshua. Hoshea means "salvation" (the Hebrew spelling of Hosea is identical), and Joshua means, "the LORD is salvation." According to Exodus 6:3 the name, "the LORD" (Hebrew, "Yahweh"), was not revealed until after the birth of Joshua; so he could not have been called "Joshua" at his birth.

2. *Moses' instructions to the spies* (13:17–20)

Moses assembled the spies and told them to go up through the "Negev" ("southward," KJV; the word means "to be dry/parched" and designates the area bordering Judah on the south) into the "hill country" ("mountain," KJV; another designation of the Negev). He instructed them to gather information about the land, the people, the towns, the fortifications, the soil, and the vegetation. He also asked them to bring back some of the fruit of the land (13:18–20). Such information was vital for making their plans for attack and for knowing what kind of land they would be possessing. He told them to "do your best" (v. 20; "be of good courage," KJV, RSV; "be bold," JB; "make an effort," NASB). As it was the season for the first ripe grapes, the time was the middle or end of July.

3. *The investigation and report of the spies* (13:21–29)

The spies explored the region from the Desert of Zin (southwest of the southern end of the Dead Sea) as far as Rehob (west of Hermon in the north; called Beth Rehob, 2 Sam. 10:6) toward Lebo Hamath (about sixty miles further north-northeast of Rehob near the Orontes river; 13:21). In other words, they searched out the entire land from north to south that God had given them.

Their reconnaisance brought them to Hebron, about twenty miles south of Jerusalem, where descendants of Anak lived (13:22; cf. Deut. 2:10). The word "Anak" means "neck" and reflects their reputation for being of great height (long-necked). A historical footnote adds that Hebron had been built seven years before Zoan in Egypt (13:22). Zoan (also known as Tanis) was a city of great antiquity. It was built before 2000 B.C., and rebuilt around 1300 B.C.

When the spies reached the Valley of Eshcol (the word means "cluster"; probably near Hebron, the area is noted for its vineyards even today), they cut off a branch bearing a single cluster of grapes. It was so large that it required two men to carry it on a pole between them (13:23). They also gathered other kinds of fruit to take back with them. After forty days they returned to where the Israelites were encamped at Kadesh (vv. 25–26).

They reported to Moses, Aaron, and the assembled Israelites and showed them the fruit (13:26). They described the land as flowing with milk and honey (v. 27; an expression found frequently in the Old Testament to describe great fertility). But they quickly added that the inhabitants were powerful and that the cities were large and well-fortified (v. 28). They reported that a mixed population of Amalekites (cf. Exod. 17:8–16; 1 Sam. 15:1–33), Hittites (cf. Gen. 15:20; 23:10), Jebusites (cf. 2 Sam. 5:6–9), Amorites (a name used of the inhabitants of Canaan as a whole and difficult to distinguish from Canaanites), and Canaanites lived in various regions of the land (13:29). Scholars have confirmed that the description here is an accurate one of the land before the conquest.

4. The spies' recommendation (13:30–33)

The spies' report created consternation among the people. Caleb (his name means "dog") silenced them and insisted that they should go up and take the land. There was no doubt in his mind that it could be accomplished (13:30). Joshua agreed with Caleb, though he is not mentioned until later (14:6–9).

The other ten spies disagreed and brought a "majority report." They insisted that the people should not attack the inhabitants, who were much stronger (13:31). They even brought an evil report concerning the land. They said it "devours those living in it" (v. 32). They did not mean cannibals lived there but that the land did not produce sufficiently to support them (cf. Ezek. 36:13–15). The dangers and anticipated difficulties they would meet would destroy them. They added that the inhabitants were of giant stature. They reported seeing Nephilim there (ancestors of Anak; Gen. 6:4, says they were on earth when the offspring were born of the union of the sons of God and daughters of men). By comparison the spies felt as small and helpless as grasshoppers (13:33; cf. Isa. 40:22).

B. The reaction to the spies' report (14:1–45)

1. The people's complaint (14:1–4)

The spies' report so terrified the people that they wept into the night (14:1). Deuteronomy 1:28 (RSV, NASB) adds that the description of Canaan caused their hearts to melt. They grumbled against Moses and Aaron (cf. Exod. 15:24; 17:3). Again they wished they had never left Egypt (14:2; cf. Exod. 14:11–12; 16:3; 17:3). They could not understand why God had brought them to a place where only destruction awaited them and their families. Deuteronomy 1:27 adds that the people said the reason the Lord brought them to Canaan was that He hated them. They concluded that it would be better to choose a new leader (literally, "give a head") and return to Egypt (14:4). Nehemiah 9:17 preserves a tradition that they did actually choose another leader. Slavery under Pharaoh with some measure of security seemed preferable to freedom under God with its uncertainties and responsibilities.

2. The appeal of Joshua and Caleb (14:5–9)

Overwhelmed by shame and sorrow, Moses and Aaron fell on their faces before the people (14:5). Joshua and Caleb tore their clothes (a common expression of grief) and denied the false report of the other spies. They reasoned with the people that the land they had explored was good and that if God was pleased with them, He would give the land to them (vv. 6–8). They exhorted the people not to rebel against the Lord and not to be afraid of the inhabitants of the land. "We will swallow them up" (v. 9; literally, "they are our bread"). They encouraged them that the enemy's protection (literally, "shadow") was gone. There was no reason to be afraid, for the Lord was with Israel.

3. God's anger (14:10–12)

Their appeals were in vain. The people talked about stoning them (14:10; the punishment for blasphemy; cf. Lev. 24:15–16; 1 Sam. 30:6). Suddenly the glory[1] of the Lord appeared at the Tent of Meeting. First seen in the desert (Exod. 16:10) and then on Mount Sinai (Exod. 24:16–18), the glory of the Lord in the Old Testament was a visible manifestation of God's presence. In later Judaism it came to be known as the Shekinah (from a word "to dwell"; "tabernacle" is from the same word) and was associated with light or radiance.

Angrily, the Lord asked how long the people would continue to treat Him with contempt (14:11; "provoke me," KJV; "despise me," RSV; "insult me," JB; cf. Exod. 10:3; 16:28; Jer. 23:26; Hos. 8:5). How long would they refuse to believe in Him, in spite of all the miraculous signs He had performed among them (14:11; cf. John 12:37)? Without faith, they could not be the people of God (cf. Heb. 11:6).

Then, for the second time, God announced that He would destroy the Israelites and make of Moses an even greater nation (14:12; cf.

---

[1]"Glory" comes from a Hebrew word meaning "to be heavy." It came to mean "honor" (e.g., Exod. 20:12). The link between "honor" and "heavy" can be traced to the ancient Near Eastern world, where a heavy person was obviously affluent because only wealthy people had enough to eat. Because of his wealth, he was respected and honored by the community. God reveals His glory (i.e., reveals His attributes that merit honor; cf. Isa. 40:5; 60:2). He also requires that His people give glory to Him (i.e., honor Him; cf. 1 Sam. 6:5).

Exod. 32:10). He would surely fulfill the promise He had made to Abraham (Gen. 12:2–3), but there would be a delay.

4. *Moses' intercession* (14:13–19)

Even as he had rejected a similar tempting offer at Sinai of elevation at the expense of his people (Exod. 32:11–14), so again Moses pleaded with the Lord not to destroy them. In a bold appeal to God's reputation, he reminded Him that the Egyptians would hear about the debacle in the desert. They already knew of His power and presence with Israel and feared Him. Now, however, if He destroyed His own people, other nations would not understand it as an act of judgment. They would say that God did not have the power to bring them into the land as He promised and therefore killed them in the desert (14:13–16; cf. Isa. 52:5; Ezek. 36:22–23). Moses probably meant that people would conclude the Canaanite deities were stronger, as wars in the ancient world were considered to be, above all, struggles between rival deities. In an almost unprecedented act of boldness, Moses challenged the Lord that His honor was at stake.

Moses suggested that God's real power could be shown not by killing His people but by His patience, love, and forgiveness (14:17–18; cf. Exod. 34:6–7). At the same time Moses acknowledged that God must act justly by punishing sin. However, he argued that God's justice did not require extinction of the people but rather a penalty, the effects of which would be limited to the third and fourth generations (14:18). Moses appealed for forgiveness (from a Hebrew word, "to send away," or "to sprinkle," i.e., "to cleanse ceremonially") on the basis of God's great love and past forgiveness from the time they left Egypt (v. 19).

5. *God's response* (14:20–35)

God answered Moses' petition by forgiving the people, i.e., not destroying all of them as He had threatened (14:20; cf. Ps. 106:23; Jer. 15:1 for Moses' efficacy as an intercessor). At the same time He took a solemn oath to destroy those who had offended Him. He prefaced the oath with "as surely as I live." This statement was based on the surest known fact in Israelite experience and underscored the certainty of fulfillment of the vow (14:21–22; cf. Isa. 49:18; Jer. 22:24; Zeph. 2:9; Heb. 6:13). He took a second oath to strengthen His threat: "As surely as the glory of the LORD fills the whole earth" (14:21; cf. comments on v. 10).

Many Israelites had complained that they did not want to go to the Promised Land; so the Lord gave them their desire. We should always be careful what we ask for; the Lord may give it to us! Not a person among those who had disobeyed and tested Him "ten times"[2] and who had witnessed His miracles in Egypt and in the desert would enter the land (14:22).

No one who had treated Him with contempt would see Canaan (v. 23). The Lord added that because Caleb had a different spirit ("a different attitude," TEV), Caleb would enter the land; and his descendants would inherit it (14:24; cf. Josh. 14:6–15 for his inheritance at Hebron). Joshua is not mentioned here, but he was allowed to enter Canaan (cf. 14:30; 32:12; Deut. 1:36, 38) because he also had demonstrated his willingness to follow the Lord to possess the land.

God then ordered Moses to lead the people back in the direction of the Red Sea (literally, "Sea of Reeds") from which they had come. If they continued northward, they would encounter the Amalekites and Canaanites (14:25). They had forfeited God's help; and if they attempted to take the land by force now, they would be defeated.

Amplifying His original pronouncement, the Lord said that every person counted in the census of twenty years of age or more (cf. 1:3) and who had grumbled against Him would die in the desert. Only Caleb, Joshua, and the children, whom the people feared would be taken as plunder, would enter the land and enjoy it (14:29–31). The Levites must have been excluded from the punishment also as they were not counted in the census mentioned in 14:29 (cf. 1:47–49; 4:1–49).

Sin always affects the innocent. Even the children would be forced to live a nomadic life in the desert for forty years while their rebellious parents were dying (14:33; cf. Exod. 20:5; Ezek. 18). The Lord reminded them that the forty years of punishment represented one year for each day they had spied out the land (14:34; cf. Deut. 2:14; Ezek. 4:4–8). They would suffer for their unfaithfulness (14:33; literally, "acts of prostitution"; cf. Jer. 3:2) and know God's "displeasure" (14:34, RSV; "breach of promise," KJV; "opposition," NASB; cf. Heb. 3:17–19).

6. *Judgment on the spies* (14:36–38)

The ten spies who had returned with the unfavorable report that

---

[2]The Talmud says there were exactly ten times that the people tested the Lord: Exodus 14:11; 15:23; 16:3; 16:20, 27; 17:2; 32:1–4; Numbers 11:4; 13:31; Psalm 106:7. In the symbolic use of numbers in the Bible, however, "ten" is a number of fullness or completeness and could mean here "many times" or "frequently."

initiated the people's rebellion were struck down with a plague and died "before the LORD" (14:37). Only two of the spies, Joshua and Caleb, survived (v. 38).

7. Defeat by the Amalekites and Canaanites (14:39–45)

When Moses told the people what their fate was to be, they began to mourn bitterly. The next day, instead of turning south as they had been ordered, they faced the high hill country ahead of them. They acknowledged their sin and determined to enter Canaan (14:39–40). Israel discovered, however, that sometimes it is too late to be sorry and too late to do the Lord's will. Moses warned them that their new resolve was actually "disobeying the LORD's command" (v. 41; literally, "passing over the Lord's mouth"). Therefore, it would not succeed. Failure was certain because the Lord was not now with them. If they attacked the Amalekites and Canaanites, they would be disastrously defeated (vv. 42–43).

In spite of the warning the Israelites set out "presumptuously" (JB; "heedlessly," NASB; "recklessly," NEB) toward the high hill country. Neither Moses nor the ark of the covenant left the camp with them (14:44). As Moses had warned, the enemy came down and defeated them, pursuing (from a word, "hammer to pieces") them all the way to Hormah (v. 45; from a word, "devotion," i.e., "dedicated to complete destruction"). Hormah's location is uncertain, but scholars believe it may have been in the region of Beersheba.

C. Additional laws and regulations (15:1–41)

Chapter 15 is composed of five sections, each dealing with some ritual practice of the Israelite religion. They have little or no connection with one another nor with the narrative that precedes or follows.

1. Grain offerings and drink offerings (15:1–16)

The regulations given here state the proper quantities of grain, oil, and wine to be presented with the burnt or fellowship offerings (cf. Lev. 1:3–17; 3:1–17). The regulations in these verses did not replace the grain offering (Lev. 2:1–16) as a separate ritual, but were concerned only with the amounts of flour, oil, and wine to be brought with the burnt offerings and fellowship offerings. The new regulations were not to take effect until after the people entered Canaan (15:2).

When they brought their burnt offerings or sacrifices (i.e., fellowship offerings) from the herd or the flock for special vows, freewill offerings, or festival offerings, the animal to be offered had to be accompanied by a grain offering of a tenth of an ephah of fine flour (about two quarts) mixed with a fourth of a hin of oil (about one quart; 15:3–4). A lamb brought for a burnt offering or sacrifice was to be accompanied by a fourth of a hin of wine as a drink offering (v. 5). The drink offering is not explained elsewhere in the Old Testament. The quantities were increased when the size of the animal was increased (a ram, vv. 6–7; a young bull, vv. 8–10).

The animal was to be offered as "an aroma pleasing to the LORD" (15:10). The phrase originated in a more ancient time when it was believed that the deity derived pleasure from inhaling the smoke of the burning flesh that ascended into his nostrils.

These regulations were not only for the native-born Israelites but also for any aliens living among them (cf. on 9:14). There was to be no difference in the laws and regulations for the Israelites and the aliens who lived among them (15:13–16).

2. An offering of the first of the ground meal (15:17–21)

These verses contain a special case of the law of firstfruits which was to be observed after Israel entered the land (cf. also chap. 18). The regulation itself is mentioned elsewhere only twice (Neh. 10:37; Ezek. 44:30). In celebration of eating for the first time food that was grown in the land, they were asked to present a portion of it as an offering to the Lord (15:19; "a heave offering," KJV). It was to be a cake (in Hebrew, *challah*, i.e., "a perforated cake") from the first of the ground meal taken from the threshing floor (v. 20). Throughout all generations the same offering was to be brought from the first portion of their ground meal (v. 21). The offering is still called the Challah. It is baked at home and thrown into the fire, as there are no priests to whom it can be taken.

3. Atonement for unintentional sins (15:22–31)

If the entire congregation were guilty of breaking any of the laws unintentionally ("by ignorance," KJV), provision was made for atonement (from a word, "to cover"). The whole community was to offer a young bull for a burnt offering, along with the prescribed grain offering and drink offering, and a male goat for a sin offering (15:22–24). The people would be forgiven because the wrong was unintentional (v. 26).

If the unintentional sin involved only one person, he was to bring a year-old female goat as a sin offering. The same regulation applied to the native-born Israelite and to the alien (15:27–29; cf. Lev. 4:1–35; 5:5–13 for other laws related to unintentional sins).

However, if a person sinned "defiantly" ("presumptuously," KJV; "with a high hand," RSV; "deliberately," JB), there was no provision for atonement for that one (15:30; cf. Mark 3:28–29). His actions showed that he despised the Lord's word (cf. 2 Sam. 12:9). Therefore, he was cut off from his people (cf. comments on 9:13), and his guilt remained on him (15:31).

4. Punishment for work on the Sabbath (15:32–36)

While in the desert, a man was discovered gathering wood on the Sabbath (15:32; cf. Exod. 20:8–11; 35:3; Lev. 24:10–23). He was brought to Moses, Aaron, and the whole assembly and placed in custody until it could be determined what should be done to him (15:33–34). As the death penalty had already been prescribed for such an offense (cf. Exod. 31:14–15; 35:2), the people were waiting to know how he should be executed.

The Lord's reply was not long in coming. The death penalty by stoning outside the camp was pronounced on the man (15:35). The entire assembly took him outside the camp and carried out the sentence, as the Lord had commanded Moses (v. 36). Sabbath harshness was not an invention of the Pharisees (cf. John 9:16). Perhaps the story of the unfortunate man was placed here to illustrate the fate of anyone who sinned defiantly (cf. 15:30–31).

5. Tassels on the garments (15:37–41)

The Lord told Moses to instruct the people to put tassels on the corners ("fringes in the borders," KJV) of their garments. The tassels were to be attached to the garment with a blue cord (15:38; cf. Deut. 22:12; Mark 6:56). They were not superstitious charms but ornaments intended to catch the attention of the eye and to serve as a reminder to be faithful (cf. a crucifix or fish necklace worn by Christians). By looking at these tassels, the people would be reminded of all the commands of the Lord that they must obey. This reminder would warn them not to prostitute themselves by following the lusts and desires of their own hearts. By remembering to obey all the Lord's commands, they would be consecrated to Him (15:40). The basis for this appeal to faithfulness was "I am the LORD your God" (v. 41).

The orthodox Jew still wears an oblong piece of cloth with a hole in the middle for passing over the head and a tassel at each corner to fulfill this command. The garment is called a tallith (cf. Matt. 9:20; 14:36; 23:5; Mark 6:56; Luke 8:44).

For Further Study

1. In a Bible dictionary or encyclopedia (see bibliography) read articles on Kadesh, atonement, Caleb, and Joshua.

2. Make a study of "the glory of the Lord" in the Bible.

3. Was God just in requiring innocent children to remain in the desert for forty years because of the sins of their parents?

4. Why are parents sometimes unwilling to trust their children's lives into the Lord's hands and purposes?

5. Make a study of Sabbath worship in the Bible and in Judaism.

Chapter 5

The Wanderings in the Desert—II
(Numbers 16:1–19:22)

God had given Moses to the Israelites as their leader. The seal of divine approval was clearly on him. He had successfully contested Pharaoh's oppression of the people and led them out of the land of bondage. His prayers had brought guidance and provision when needed. His intercession had saved them from God's wrath on more than one occasion. However, in spite of repeated evidences of God's blessing on him, the people challenged and resisted his leadership all along the way. Their rebellious spirit was not broken, either by divine love or by divine chastisement.

A. Rebellion among the people (16:1–50)

1. *Leaders of the rebellion* (16:1–2)

Korah, a member of the Levite family that was later associated with the temple choirs (cf. Pss. 42–49), was joined by three members of the Reubenite family (Dathan, Abiram, and On) in a rebellion against Moses (16:1). They were joined by 250 well-known community leaders (v. 2).[1]

2. *Korah's rebellion* (16:3–11)

The rebels challenged Moses, saying, "You have gone too far! (16:3; "Ye take too much upon you," KJV; literally, "Enough for you"). Like the true demagogue who poses as a champion of the common people, Korah insisted that Moses should not enjoy a privileged position, as all

---

[1]Cf. George Buchanan Gray, *A Critical and Exegetical Commentary on Numbers*, The International Critical Commentary, (Edinburgh: T. & T. Clark, 1903), pp. 186–88, for arguments that stories of different revolts have been combined into one narrative in this chapter.

the people were holy. Moses fell face forward on the ground, either in an attitude of despair or of prayer (v. 4). He proposed a test to show who had been chosen for divine service (literally, "He will cause to come near to him," v. 5). He told the rebels to bring censers before the Lord the next day, filled with fire and incense (v. 18 adds at "the Tent of Meeting"). There the Lord would choose who was set apart for His service. Moses hurled their own accusation back at them, saying, "You Levites have gone too far!" (v. 7).

He told the Levites in general and Korah in particular that it was a sufficient honor for the Lord to separate them for ministry at the tabernacle (16:9). He accused them of trying to usurp the priesthood also (v. 10). He added that their rebellion was against the Lord, not against Aaron, as Aaron was not a self-appointed priest. He had received his office from God (16:11; cf. Exod. 16:7).

3. *The rebellion of Dathan and Abiram* (16:12–14)

Moses summoned Dathan and Abiram, but they refused to come (16:12). They accused Moses of wanting to lord it over them (v. 13; "make yourself a prince over us," RSV; cf. Exod. 2:14). They said Moses had brought them *out of* a land of "milk and honey" (not *into* it; the only time this phrase is used of Egypt; cf. "a land of olive trees and honey" to describe Assyria, 2 Kings 18:32). They reminded Moses that he had failed to bring them into the land (ignoring the fact that they had refused to enter it). They suspected that Moses wanted to gouge out their eyes if they appeared before him (16:14). The phrase "gouge out" can be understood figuratively, i.e., to hoodwink or blind them by false promises. It actually was a cruel punishment inflicted on a defeated enemy in ancient times (cf. Judg. 16:21; 1 Sam. 11:2; 2 Kings 25:7).

4. *Punishment of the rebels* (16:15–35)

Their impudence angered Moses. Instead of interceding for them, he asked the Lord not to accept their offering. He denied that he had ever abused his power by taking a gift from them or wronging any of them (16:15; cf. 1 Sam. 12:3). Moses then ordered Korah and his followers to appear before the Lord the next day with their censers filled with incense. Aaron would also be there with his censer (16:16–17). When they all gathered the next day as instructed, the glory of the Lord appeared to the entire assembly (cf. comments on 14:10). The

Lord angrily told Moses and Aaron to remove themselves so that He could destroy all the rebels on the spot (16:19–21).

As he had done on similar occasions in the past, Moses, now joined by Aaron, pleaded with God not to destroy the entire assembly because of the sin of one person (16:22). The Lord responded by telling Moses to order the people away from the tents of Korah, Dathan, and Abiram (v. 24). The people did as Moses instructed them, while the rebels stood defiantly in front of their tents with their families (v. 27).

Moses then announced what was going to happen to show that the Lord had appointed him as leader. If the rebels died a natural death (i.e., if no punishment were forthcoming), it would prove that the Lord had not appointed Moses. However, if He did something "totally new" (literally, "create a creation"; cf. Jer. 31:22) by causing the earth to open and swallow them alive, all would know that they had treated the Lord with contempt (16:28–30). Even as Moses finished speaking, the ground under them split apart. Korah and his household went down alive with all their possessions into the grave of the dead ("into the pit," KJV; "into Sheol," RSV; the name of the abode of the dead in the ancient Near East; cf. Gen. 37:35; Job 10:21–22; 24:19–20; 30:23; Pss. 6:5; 115:17; Eccl. 9:10; Isa. 14:9–11; 38:18 for Old Testament attitudes toward Sheol). From Numbers 26:11 we learn that not all the family of Korah was destroyed. When the people saw what had happened, they fled in terror to escape the same fate (16:34). Fire from the Lord consumed the 250 men who had joined Korah in the rebellion (16:35; cf. Jude 11).

5. A sign for the people (16:36–40)

The Lord instructed Moses to tell Eleazar to take the rebels' censers and scatter the coals from them at a distance from the tent. Then the censers were to be hammered into sheets to overlay the altar. Thus, they would always be a visible sign to the Israelites and a reminder that no one who was not descended from Aaron should draw near to offer incense to the Lord (16:36–38; cf. 2 Chron. 26:16–21). As the altar of incense was covered with gold (Exod. 30:3) and the altar of burnt offering was overlaid with bronze when they were made (Exod. 38:2), it is uncertain which altar was intended here.

6. Punishment of the people (16:41–50)

The fate of the rebels should have silenced the rest of the people once and for all, but they turned on Moses and Aaron and accused them of killing "the LORD's people" (16:41). The glory of the Lord suddenly appeared again at the Tent of Meeting. The Lord told Moses to separate himself from the people so that He could kill them at once (v. 45). Moses quickly instructed Aaron to take his censer filled with incense, along with fire from the altar, and go immediately to the people to make atonement for them, lest they all be killed by a plague that had already begun (v. 46). The incident reminds us that blood was not the only way of making atonement. Aaron did as Moses instructed him, standing "between the living and the dead" (v. 48). The plague was stopped but not before 14,700 of the people died (v. 49).

The experience served to show Israel that incense offered by unauthorized persons brought death, whereas it was acceptable to the Lord and efficacious when brought by an authorized priest.

B. The budding of Aaron's rod (17:1–13)

Because Aaron's authority had been challenged as well as that of Moses, the Lord determined to offer the people convincing proof of the legitimacy of the Aaronic priesthood. He told Moses to tell the people to bring twelve staffs ("rods," KJV, RSV). One from the leader of each tribe was to be brought, with his name written on his staff (17:2; "staff" and "tribe" are from the same Hebrew word). Aaron's name was to be written on the staff of the family of Levi (v. 3). All the staffs were then to be placed before the Testimony (i.e., the ark of the covenant). The staff of the man whom God had chosen as priest would sprout and so the complaints of the people should end once and for all (vv. 4–5)

The leaders did as Moses instructed them, and he placed their staffs before the Lord in the Tent of the Testimony (17:6–7). The next day Moses entered the tent and saw that Aaron's staff had not only sprouted but had budded, blossomed, and produced almonds! (cf. Jer. 1:11). He brought all the staffs out for the people to see and gave each leader his staff (17:8–9). The Lord instructed Moses to return Aaron's staff to its place in front of the ark to be preserved as a sign for the rebellious Israelites of future generations (17:10; cf. Heb. 9:4).

Such a miraculous proof was intended to end the people's murmurings once and for all. It should have, but it did not. They began to grumble and cry out in fear that all of them would surely die (17:12–13). They now feared that even coming near the tabernacle could result in their death.

C. Wages and duties of the priests and Levites (18:1–32)

This chapter is a logical sequel to chapter 17 that vindicated the Aaronic priesthood. It clarifies the wages and duties of the priests and Levites and adds a valuable contribution to their history.

1. Duties (18:1–7)

The Lord usually instructed Aaron through Moses, but here and on one other occasion Aaron was addressed directly (18:1; cf. Lev. 10:8). The Lord reminded him that he and his family were responsible for any offenses against the sanctuary or the priesthood. If their negligence brought about any kind of profanation of the tabernacle, such as an unauthorized entrance, the consequences would be on them.

Furthermore, the Lord made clear the distinction in the duties of the priests and the Levites (18:2–4). The Levites were a "gift" to the priests to assist them in the work of the tabernacle. They were to do what the priests asked but could not go near the sacred furnishings of the sanctuary or the altar. If they did, both they and the priests would be put to death. Only the priests could enter the tabernacle or minister at the altar. Anyone else who came near the sanctuary would be put to death (18:5–7).

2. Offerings due the priests (18:8–20)

Verses 8–32 list the various kinds of remuneration due the priests and Levites for their services on behalf of the Israelites. Verse 8 is a general statement that all the holy offerings brought by Israel belonged to the priests, but the verses that follow add some limitations. They were to have all grain, sin, and guilt offerings except for those parts that were required to be burned on the altar. These offerings could be eaten by any male member of the priestly families (vv. 9–10). In addition, whatever was set aside from the gifts of the wave offerings could be eaten by male and female members of the priestly families who were ceremonially clean (18:11; cf. Lev. 22:3–8).

Also, all the best (literally, "all fat") of the olive oil, new wine, and grain that the people brought of the firstfruits of their harvest could be eaten by members of the priestly families who were ceremonially clean (18:12–13). Two different terms are used for "firstfruits" in these verses; it is not certain whether a technical distinction is intended or not.[2]

---

[2]Ibid., pp. 224–29, for a lengthy discussion of the Hebrew words for firstfruits used in 18:12–13.

Everything "devoted," or dedicated, to the Lord belonged to the priests (18:14; cf. Lev. 27:28–29). This included the firstborn of all animals offered to the Lord, except for the blood and fat, which belonged to the Lord. Provision was made for redemption with money of the firstborn son and for the firstborn male of unclean animals (18:15–18; cf. Exod. 13:12–13; Lev. 11; 27:11–13). The Lord promised all these things to the priests and their families as an "everlasting covenant of salt" (18:19; an inviolable covenant; the expression was perhaps derived from salt's preservative quality; cf. 2 Chron. 13:5). The priests received their support from the people's sacred gifts, as they did not share in the inheritance of the land (cf. 26:62; Josh. 14:3–4). The Lord was their inheritance (18:20; cf. Deut. 10:9; Josh. 13:14).

3. The tithe for the Levites (18:21–24)

The Lord designated all the tithes in Israel as the inheritance of the Levites in return for the service they rendered Him at the Tent of Meeting (18:21; cf. Lev. 27:30–33; Deut. 14:22–29; 26:12; 2 Chron. 31:6). Their service involved personal risk (18:22–23). Like the priests, they received no territorial inheritance among the tribes (v. 24).

4. Additional payment to the priests (18:25–32)

The Levites received a tithe, but they were also required to pay a tithe to the priests of what they received (18:26). Their tithes were "reckoned," or considered (the same word, rendered "credited," is used of Abraham, Gen. 15:6), as though they came from their own threshing floors and winepresses (18:27). They were cautioned to bring as the Lord's portion only the best and holiest part of everything that had been given to them (18:29; cf. Mal. 1:7–8, 12–14). Whatever remained could be eaten by the Levites and their households, for it was their wages for the work they did at the Tent of Meeting. Again they were cautioned to bring only the best to the Lord, lest they defile the holy offerings and die (18:31–32).

The regulations of this chapter clearly established the principle that those who were unable to earn their own livelihood by reason of their dedication to the Lord's service were to be supported by the offerings the people brought to the Lord (cf. Luke 10:7; 1 Tim. 5:18).

D. The rite of the red heifer (19:1–22)

This chapter does not seem to be related to what precedes or follows.

It deals with a single subject—pollution through contact with the dead and how that pollution was to be removed. The law given here is presupposed in 31:19–24 and is mentioned in Hebrews 9:13. It would have been appropriate to include it with Leviticus 11–16. Other regulations governing contact with the dead are found in 6:9–11 and Leviticus 5:1–6; 11:24–28, 31–47; 22:4–8. This particular rite puzzled the Jewish people. There is a tradition that even King Solomon with all his wisdom despaired of learning its secret meaning. Another tradition says the rite was performed only seven times, once by Moses, once by Ezra, and five times since Ezra.

1. *Instructions for slaughter of the heifer* (19:1–10)

The animal required for this rite was a red heifer (19:2; "red cow," NEB; probably reddish-brown, as no unnatural color was intended). It could have no blemish, such as blindness, lameness, or disease (cf. Lev. 22:22–24). The rabbis said that two hairs of another color would disqualify it! It could never have been yoked, i.e., used for some secular purpose (19:2; cf. 1 Sam. 6:7).

The heifer was to be given to Eleazar (perhaps so that Aaron would not be defiled), taken outside the camp, and slaughtered in his presence (19:3; cf. Heb. 13:11–12). He was to take some of its blood on his finger and sprinkle it seven times (the number of completeness) toward the front of the Tent of Meeting. The direction of sprinkling probably indicated that the heifer belonged to the Lord. Then the animal was to be completely burned, even its blood. While it burned, the priest was to throw cedar wood, hyssop, and scarlet wool into the fire. The commentaries differ as to the significance and purpose of these items. Their exact significance cannot be determined. After that, the priest and the person who burned the animal were to wash their clothes and bathe themselves. Then they could reenter the camp but were ceremonially unclean until evening (19:4–8; cf. Lev. 16:26, 28).

A ceremonially clean person was required to gather up the ashes of the heifer and place them in a ceremonially clean place outside the camp. The ashes were available to the community for use in the "water of cleansing" as purification from sin ("water of separation," KJV; "water for impurity," RSV; "water of ritual purification," NEB). The man who gathered the ashes was also required to wash his clothes, and he, too, remained unclean until evening (19:9–10).

2. *Purification for defilement by a corpse* (19:11–19)

If a person touched a corpse (Hebrew, *nephesh;* the word is traditionally translated as "soul"; e.g., Gen. 2:7, KJV) he was considered unclean for seven days. "Seven" probably emphasized the serious nature of the defilement. He was required to purify himself with water that was sprinkled on him on the third and seventh days in order to become ceremonially clean. If he did not observe the ritual, he remained unclean (19:11–12). Anyone who touched a corpse and did not purify himself defiled the tabernacle because he remained unclean. Such a person was to be cut off from Israel (v. 13; cf. comments on 9:13; cf. Exod. 12:15; Lev. 7:20).

When a person died in a tent (i.e., a dwelling), anyone who entered that tent or was in it at the time of death would be unclean for seven days. It was not actually necessary to touch the corpse to become unclean. Every open container in the tent without a lid fastened on it was also unclean (19:14).

Anyone who touched a corpse outdoors was unclean for seven days, and this was true whether the person had died violently by the sword or by a natural death. The touching of a human bone or a grave also made a person unclean for the same period of time (19:16). In later times graves were whitewashed so they could be clearly seen, and thus accidental defilement was avoided (cf. Matt. 23:27; Luke 11:44; Acts 23:3).

The person who had become unclean through any of the circumstances enumerated above was required to submit to the ceremony of purification. Some of the ashes of the red heifer that had been preserved were put in a jar and "fresh water" was poured over them (19:17; "running water," KJV, RSV; literally, "living water"). A ceremonially clean person took hyssop, dipped it in the water, and sprinkled the tent, the furnishings, and all the people who were in it. The same was done for anyone who had touched a human bone, a grave, or a person who had been killed or had died a natural death (v. 18). The sprinkling was done on the third and seventh days. The person being cleansed was then required to wash his clothes and bathe his body. That evening he was considered once again to be clean (v. 19).

3. *Punishment for ignoring the purification law* (19:20–22)

The warning of 19:13 was repeated, perhaps for solemn emphasis. The person who did not purify himself was cut off from the community

(19:20; cf. 9:13). The person who sprinkled the water for cleansing on the unclean person was required to wash his clothes. Anyone who touched the water itself was considered unclean until evening. The water cleansed the unclean person but defiled the clean person who touched it. Anything touched by the unclean person became unclean, and anyone who touched the object that had been made unclean was also unclean until evening (19:21–22). Uncleanness was considered to be highly contagious in Israel (cf. Hag. 2:13).

For Further Study

1. In a Bible dictionary or encyclopedia (see bibliography) read articles on incense, Sheol, and tithe.

2. What are legitimate evidences that a person has truly been authorized by God to be a minister for Him?

3. Are there any indisputable "proofs" of God's reality that would stop the mouths of unbelievers?

4. Are Christians bound to pay the tithe?

Chapter 6

The Journey From Paran to Moab
(Numbers 20:1–21:35)

The years of Israel's punishment were drawing to an end. Most of the history of the period is unknown. The graves of an entire generation of rebellious Israelites had been dug throughout the desert terrain of Paran. A new generation was about to end the aimless wandering and begin the final stages of the journey to Canaan. The people did not attempt to reenter the land directly from the south but detoured around the territory of Edom to the plains of Moab east of Canaan. There they encamped and made their plans to cross the Jordan River and take possession of the land.

A. The end of the desert wanderings (20:1–29)

1. *The death of Miriam* (20:1)

In the first month of what was probably the fortieth year, the Israelites arrived at the Desert of Zin (20:1). The region lay adjacent to and north of Paran and included Kadesh; there they encamped. It was the same Kadesh where almost forty years earlier they had refused to enter Canaan from the south (cf. 13:26). Without any specific details, we are told only that Miriam died and was buried there.

2. *The people's complaint for water* (20:2–9)

The people were without water again, and in a confrontation that sounds very much like Exodus 17:1–7 they quarreled with Moses. They wished they had died when "our brothers fell dead before the LORD" (20:3; undoubtedly a reference to the fate of Korah and the other rebels, 16:49). They blamed Moses for their predicament. As before, they expressed a desire to have remained in Egypt (cf. comments at

14:2). There was nothing to eat and no water to drink (20:5).

Moses and Aaron took refuge at the Tent of Meeting, where the glory of the Lord appeared to them (cf. comments at 14:10). The Lord ordered Moses to take the staff and assemble the people (20:8; v. 9 makes it clear that the staff was Aaron's that had budded; cf. 17:10). The Lord told them to speak (the command is plural) to the rock, and water would come forth that would satisfy the people and their livestock (20:8).

3. Striking of the rock (20:10–13)

Moses took the staff from the Lord's presence in the tabernacle, and he and Aaron called the people together. Moses addressed them angrily: "Listen, you rebels, must we bring you water out of this rock?" (20:10). With that, he struck the rock two times with the staff. The water gushed out, and the people and their livestock eagerly satisfied their thirst (v. 11).

If the narrative had ended here, it is unlikely that the reader would have detected that Moses had done anything to anger the Lord. But the rest of the narrative makes it clear that something was wrong. The Lord told the two leaders that because they "did not trust in me enough to honor me as holy in the sight of the Israelites," they would not be allowed to lead the people into the land (20:12). The place was called Meribah (from a word that means "quarrel"; cf. Exod. 17:7).

Moses had been faithful for forty years, and there was surely no greater desire in his heart than to march into Canaan at the head of his people. Yet now he was being denied that privilege for one sin, whose seriousness is not immediately apparent. What, then, was the nature of Moses' sin that caused him to forfeit the blessing of a successful conclusion to his years of leadership?

The question is too complex for simple answers, as indicated by the many solutions scholars have proposed: (1) Moses was disobedient; he had been told to speak to the rock, but instead he struck it twice; 20:24 supports this interpretation. However, in the parallel experience of Exodus 17:1–7, God had commanded him to strike the rock (Exod. 17:6). Therefore, more than just a slight change in carrying out orders may have been involved. (2) Anger has been suggested as Moses' sin. He addressed the people as "you rebels," and by striking the rock he also displayed his anger. It was an emotion not worthy of a spiritual leader, though we are inclined to be sympathetic toward Moses in the light of all he had endured from his people. Moses was surely aware that God was not angry with them, as their complaint was legitimate and His response was positive. A divinely chosen leader must be an example at all times and cannot indulge his personal feelings. (3) Distrust of God might have been the sin; 20:12 supports this interpretation. Perhaps Moses did not believe that only speaking to the rock would be sufficient to bring forth water.

Other explanations of Moses' sin include: (4) His sin was a bitter spirit toward his people (cf. Ps. 106:33). Moses did not exhibit the gentle and patient spirit of the true shepherd, who does not beat and berate his sheep. The true shepherd "lays down his life for the sheep" (John 10:11). The modern parallel is the pastor who dislikes and criticizes his congregation. (5) Moses' sin may have been that of taking credit on himself for something that only God could do (cf. Neh. 9:15; Isa. 37:20; 48:21). In 20:10 he shouted, "Must *we* bring you water?" He seemed to be telling the people that he and Aaron were responsible for the miracle about to take place. It could be argued that "we" included God, but even so, Moses was taking some of the credit on himself. Only God could perform such a miracle, and Moses should have said so (cf. Deut. 8:17–18). (6) God was angry with all the people, but He let His punishment fall on one man vicariously, rather than on the entire community (cf. Deut. 1:37; 3:26; 4:21; Isa. 53:5–6).

Moses' sin probably included elements of all these explanations. Whatever its exact nature, the deed was serious enough to prevent Moses' completing the journey with his people.

A Jewish tradition says the water that gushed from the rock followed the people all the way to Canaan. A variant says that the rock followed them all the way, stopping when they stopped and moving when they moved. Paul gave a Christological interpretation to the anceint tradition as an illustration of the Lord's care (1 Cor. 10:4).

4. *Request for passage through Edom denied* (20:14–21)

A glance at a map will reveal that the easiest route around the south end of the Dead Sea would be through Edom and Moab. Moses chose to lead the people by this route. However, to avoid conflict with the Edomites he sent word to the king of Edom, requesting permission to pass peacefully through his land. He appealed to their kinship ("your brother Israel," 20:14). It was a relationship that went back to Jacob and Esau (cf. Gen. 25:21–26; 36:1). He reminded them of God's part in Israel's deliverance from Egypt (20:16; cf. Exod. 23:20). He promised not to disturb their fields or vineyards or to drink water from their wells (20:17). They would stay on the king's highway (a public road or regular caravan route) until they passed through the territory of Edom.

The Edomites responded by refusing Moses' request, and they threatened military action if the Israelites made an attempt to pass through their land (20:18). They reinforced their threat by assembling a large army (v. 20). The Israelites decided not to risk a confrontation and turned another way, going around the southern extremity of Edom (v. 21).

5. *The death of Aaron* (20:22–29)

Israel journeyed from Kadesh to Mount Hor (20:22). The location of this mountain is unknown, although traditionally it is believed to be near Petra (specifically, Jebel Harun, fifty miles south of the Dead Sea). However, that would place it in the middle of Edom, which is certainly incorrect, as the text says it was "near the border of Edom" (v. 23). Modern scholars have proposed Jebel Madurah, not far from Kadesh and on the northwest of the Edomite border, as its site.

At Mount Hor the Lord announced that Aaron would die there (20:24; "be gathered to his people"; cf. Gen. 25:8; 35:29; 49:33; Judg. 2:10; 2 Kings 22:20; the phrase was originally a reference to the family sepulcher where its members were entombed; later it took on overtones of some kind of belief in afterlife). He was denied the privilege of entering the Promised Land because of his part in Moses' rebellion at Meribah (cf. 20:10–12). Aaron's sin seems to have been the sin of omission. He knew what the Lord had instructed Moses to do. He should have protested when Moses struck the rock, but he did nothing. His silence made him a party to the sin.

At the Lord's command Moses, Aaron, and Eleazar went to the top of the mountain in view of the whole community. Moses removed Aaron's priestly garments and put them on Eleazar (20:28; cf. Exod. 29:29–37; Lev. 8:7–9). There Aaron died. The place of Aaron's death is given elsewhere as Moserah (Deut. 10:6), which may have been the name of a particular location in the vicinity of Mount Hor.

When Moses and Eleazar returned, the people mourned Aaron's death for thirty days (20:29; cf. Deut. 34:8 and also note other similarities to Moses' death).

Some important lessons can be learned from the events of chapter 20: (1) Even the most faithful Christian should never become overconfident that he will not fail God. (2) A person may, like Moses, be a blessing to others but miss a blessing for himself because of sin. (3) The privilege of leadership carries a heavy responsibility; God holds that person to greater accountability. (4) God expects unquestioning obedience to His commands. (5) A spiritual leader must be a good example at all times. (6) Sins of omission can be as serious as sins of commission.

B. Final events before reaching Moab (21:1–35)

1. *Defeat of the king of Arad* (21:1–3)

This passage has caused some difficulties because at the close of chapter 20 the Israelites were moving southward to go around Edom. Here they are found fighting far to the north at Arad, a well-fortified settlement that has been identified with modern Tell Arad, about eight miles south of Hebron. The narrative can best be explained as an abortive attempt to cross the Arabah just to the south of the Dead Sea. Recent excavations at Arad have produced the significant discovery of a sanctuary where the Lord was worshiped (other than at Jerusalem) throughout the period of the monarchy.

The Canaanite king of Arad heard of the Israelite approach along the road to Atharim (identified by some as Tamar or Hazazon-tamar, a few miles south of the Dead Sea, and by others as the name of a caravan route). He attacked the Israelites and captured some of them. They, in turn, asked the Lord to give the enemy into their hands and vowed to destroy their towns completely. The prayer was answered, and the victorious Israelites destroyed the attackers and their towns. They named the place Hormah (which means "devotion," i.e., dedicated to complete destruction; cf. 14:45; Josh. 12:14; Judg. 1:17). It has been identified with modern Tell el-Mishash, about ten miles east of Beersheba.

2. *The fiery serpents* (21:4–9)

The Israelites journeyed from Mount Hor (cf. 20:22) around the southern extremity of Edom toward the Red Sea (21:4; literally, "Sea of Reeds"). It was probably the Gulf of Aqabah, not the sea of the Exodus (cf. 14:25; 1 Kings 9:26). Though it was a new generation that Moses was leading, the complaining spirit was the same. The people became impatient (literally, "the soul of the people was short"; cf. Judg. 16:16, where the same expression is used of Samson). They spoke against God and Moses. They complained that they had been brought out of Egypt

only to die for lack of food and water. Furthermore, they detested the
manna, which they described as "miserable" (literally, "light" or
"worthless"; 21:5). It is suggested in 21:10 and 33:43 that they were at
Punon, identified with modern Feinan, twenty-five miles south of the
Dead Sea.

God responded to their blasphemy by sending poisonous snakes
among them (21:6; "fiery serpents," KJV; the same adjective is translated as "seraphim," literally, "burning ones," in Isa. 6:2; the word
here refers to the inflammation they caused, not to their appearance).
Many Israelites were bitten and died. The survivors acknowledged to
Moses that they had sinned "against the LORD and against you" (21:7).
They asked him to pray for the removal of the snakes. Poisonous serpents are still quite numerous in the Sinai Peninsula and the desert
regions of Judah.

Because the Lord is willing to forgive when people repent, He responded to Moses' intercession. He told Moses to make a representa-
tion of a snake, attach it to a pole, and set it up where the people could
see it. Anyone who was bitten and then looked at the serpent would
live. Moses fashioned the snake of bronze (not "brass," KJV, as it was
hardly known that early) as he had been instructed and attached it to a
pole (21:9). Those who were bitten and looked at the bronze snake did
not die.

It was not the serpent that healed by some magical power, but rather
the look of faith that brought healing (the New Testament parallel is
found in John 3:14–15). A "logical" Israelite could have reasoned that
looking at a metal serpent could not counteract the venom in his body.
His unbelief would result in his death. A believing Israelite would
acknowledge that he did not understand how the glance at the metal
snake could save him, but he would do it because God told him to do
so. His faith would save him.

The bronze serpent remained among the people and eventually became an object of idolatrous worship (2 Kings 18:4). King Hezekiah
destroyed it along with other idols the people cherished. Today the
serpent has become the symbol of healing for the medical profession,
not because of the biblical story, but through a Greek legend about
Aesculapius, the god of medicine.

3. *The journey from Oboth to Pisgah* (21:10–20)

The people continued their journey to Oboth (21:10; location unknown, but perhaps east of Edom). From there they moved on to Iye Abarim (v. 11; i.e., "ruins of Abarim"; its exact location is unknown) in the desert bordering Moab on the east side. From there they continued to the Zered Valley (v. 12; "Zared," KJV; location also unknown, but it would be north of Iye Abarim; cf. Deut. 2:13–14). Next they camped beside the Arnon River, which was the border between Moab and the Amorites (21:13; cf. Judg. 11:13). According to 21:14 a record of this encampment was preserved in the "Book of the Wars of the LORD," an otherwise unknown book.[1] The locations of Waheb, Suphah, and Ar, mentioned in verses 14–15, are all uncertain.

Then they continued to Beer (i.e., "well"; location uncertain), where the Lord provided water for them (21:16). The celebration of the discovery of water at a well they dug was preserved in what has sometimes been called the "Song of the Well" (vv. 17–18). Other stopping places included Mattanah ("gift"), Nahaliel ("God's stream"), and Bamoth ("high places"), none of which can be identified (v. 19). From Bamoth they journeyed to a valley in Moab where the top of Pisgah overlooked the "wasteland" (v. 20; understood as a proper name, "Jeshimon," KJV, NASB, NAB; cf. 1 Sam. 23:19). They had now arrived on the plains of Moab, where they could view Canaan across the Dead Sea. The years of travel were coming to an end.

4. *Encounter with Sihon, king of the Amorites* (21:21–30)

As they had done with the Edomites, the Israelites sent messengers to Sihon, king of the Amorites (also called "king of Heshbon," his chief city, Deut. 2:26), requesting permission to pass through his country. They promised not to disturb the fields or vineyards or to drink water from the wells (21:21–22; cf. the account in Deut. 2:24–37; Judg. 11:19–22). They also promised not to depart from the king's highway (cf. comments on 20:17). The land of Sihon extended from the Arnon to the Jabbok River and from the desert to the Jordan. It embraced approximately the area occupied later by Reuben and Gad (cf. 32:1–5).

Sihon denied the request and sent his army out against Israel and fought them at Jahaz (site not identified; 21:23; cf. Josh. 13:18). Israel defeated him and took over his land from the Arnon in the south to the

---

[1]Other "lost" books mentioned in the Old Testament include the Book of Jashar (Josh. 10:13; 2 Sam. 1:18), the book of the annals of Solomon (1 Kings 11:41), the book of the annals of the kings of Israel (1 Kings 14:19), and the book of the annals of the kings of Judah (1 Kings 14:29).

Jabbok in the north and as far east as the fortified Ammonite border (21:24). All the cities of the Amorites were taken, including Heshbon, the royal city (vv. 25–26; modern Hesban, about twenty miles east of the northern end of the Dead Sea). Sihon, who once had defeated the king of Moab and had taken all his land as far as the Arnon, was now himself defeated (v. 26).

At this point in the narrative an ancient poem celebrating the conquest of Moab by the Amorites is found (21:27–30; cf. Jer. 48:45). Its original author is unknown. Perhaps its inclusion here served as a satire against the Amorites—the conqueror had now become the defeated. Moab's god, Chemosh, either in anger gave his people into the hands of the Amorites or was not able to save them from the marauding Amorites (21:29). Moab was laid waste from Heshbon to Dibon all the way to Medeba (v. 30).

5. *Encounter with Og, king of Bashan* (21:31–35)

Having defeated the Amorites, Israel occupied their land (21:31). Moses sent spies to Jaazer, near the Ammonite border, to determine its strength. His armies took the town and its surrounding settlements and drove out the Amorites living there (v. 32). Then they marched toward Bashan (a fertile district east of the Jordan, noted for its forests and pastures; cf. Isa. 2:13; Amos 4:1). Og, the king of Bashan, with his army fought Israel at Edrei (probably modern Der'a, forty miles east of the Jordan). Before the opposing armies met, the Lord assured Moses that Israel would be victorious and that Og and his army should be treated as Sihon (21:34). Israel's victory was complete. There were no survivors among the enemy as the Israelites took possession of Og's land (21:35; cf. Deut. 3:1–11).

For Further Study

1. In a Bible dictionary or encyclopedia (see bibliography) read articles on the geographical locations in chapters 20–21 with which you are not familiar.

2. Make a careful study of the two accounts of the provision of water at Meribah (Exod. 17:1–7; Num. 20:1–13) to determine the similarities and differences in the narratives.

3. Was Moses' punishment for his sin at Meribah too severe?

4. How do you justify Israel's warfare that seized the territory of people already living there?

PART THREE: *Events on the Plains of Moab*

Chapter 7

The Story of Balaam
(Numbers 22:1–24:25)

Israel was encamped on the plains of Moab along the Jordan across from Jericho. Her victories over Arad, Sihon, and Og did not go unnoticed by other peoples living in the region. The Moabites were terrified that they might become the next victim of the invading horde, and therefore sought help against them. Living in a world of superstition and magic, people in the ancient world believed that the gods could be made to do their bidding and that events could be controlled by incantations, curses, and other means that today would be called "black magic" or "voodoo." Even Israel was caught up in the popular beliefs at times. However, the Old Testament makes it clear that God did not sanction these beliefs (cf. Lev. 19:26; Deut. 18:9–14). No magical rite could control Him, whether performed by an Israelite or anyone else, for He was sovereign. The story of Balaam tells about a diviner who learned that he could not control God.

A. Balak and Balaam (22:1–40)

1. *Moab's fear of Israel* (22:1–6)

Balak (his name means "one who lays waste"), king of Moab, saw all that Israel had done to the Amorites and was terrified of the horde that had invaded his land (22:2). His people shared his dread and expected to be licked up "as an ox licks up the grass of the field" (v. 4). Balak sent word to Balaam, the son of Beor, who was at Pethor near "the River" (i.e., the Euphrates) in his native land (v. 5; "the land of Amaw," RSV). Pethor has usually been identified as Pitru (Pituru) near Carchemish, four hundred miles from Moab. The Mesopotamian diviner must have had a reputation as a wonder worker to have been known so far away.

Balak informed Balaam that a people had come out of Egypt who covered the land adjoining his. He requested the soothsayer to come and put a curse on the invaders so that Balak could drive them out of the country (22:6). The practice of cursing an enemy before battle was common in the ancient world. Balak flattered Balaam by assuring him that his ability to bless and curse was well-known.

2. *Balak's first request thwarted* (22:7–14)

Midianite and Moabite elders took Balak's message to Balaam together with fees that were customary for performing divination (22:7; cf. 1 Sam. 9:8; 1 Kings 14:3; 2 Kings 8:8–9; Mic. 3:11; 2 Peter 2:15). Balaam invited them to spend the night there while he sought an answer from the Lord (22:8). His reference to the Lord does not mean that he was a true worshiper. He believed that he had the power to contact any deity to receive instructions. God did appear to Balaam that night and conversed with him. Balaam informed Him that Balak had sent messengers requesting that he curse the invading Israelites so that Balak could drive them out (vv. 9–11). The Lord ordered Balaam not to go with the messengers or to put a curse on Israel (v. 12). Balaam obediently informed Balak's princes to return home without him because the Lord had not given him permission to accompany them (v. 13). They returned to Balak with Balaam's reply (v. 14).

3. *Balak's second request* (22:15–20)

Balak did not give up. He sent princes more distinguished and numerous than the first to impress Balaam (22:15). Through the messengers he appealed again to Balaam to come help him. He promised to reward him handsomely ("load you with honours," JB) if he would curse the Israelites (vv. 16–17). Perhaps he assumed Balaam was engaging in typical Oriental bargaining and wanted more pay. Balaam emphatically rejected the offer. Even if Balak gave him a palace filled with silver and gold, he knew he was unable to overrule the command of the "Lord my God" (v. 18). In the polytheistic world of Balaam, it was easy for him to speak of the Lord in personal terms and still not imply exclusive allegiance (cf. Nebuchadnezzar, Dan. 2:47; 4:2, 34–35).

Balaam did, however, invite them to spend the night while he consulted the Lord to learn of any changes in His orders (22:19). God spoke to him and allowed him to accompany the messengers back to Balak, but He cautioned the diviner to do only what He allowed (v. 20).

4. Balaam and his donkey (22:21–35)

The next day Balaam arose, saddled his donkey, and departed with the princes of Moab (22:21). God was angry with Balaam, though the reason for His anger is unclear since He had given Balaam permission to go with the Moabites. Perhaps He was angry because Balaam did not admit to the princes that he could not curse the Israelites even if he went with them. The angel of the Lord stood in the road "to oppose him" (22:22; "for an adversary," KJV; the same Hebrew word for "Satan," mentioned by name only in the Old Testament in 1 Chron. 21:1; Job 1–2; Zech. 3:1–2; and Ps. 109:6, KJV). His sword was drawn to block their way (22:23; cf. Josh. 5:13). The donkey turned off the road into a field, whereupon Balaam beat her to force her back on the road.

The identity of the angel of the Lord has long been the subject of study by theologians. Sometimes he appears to be different from God (Exod. 23:20–23; Num. 22:22; Judg. 5:23; 6:22; 2 Sam. 24:16; Zech. 1:12–13). Sometimes the two are identical and interchangeable (Gen. 16:7–13; 22:11–12; 48:15–16; Exod. 3:2–4; Judg. 2:1; 6:11–24; 13:3–22). He is best understood as a visible manifestation of God Himself. These visible appearances of God in the Bible are called theophanies (the word means "an appearance of God"). Theophanies occur in nature (fire, Exod. 3:2; a cloud, Exod. 13:21; a storm, 1 Kings 19:11; Job 38:1), in human form (Gen. 18; Exod. 33:21–23; Isa. 6:1; Ezek. 1:26–27), but never in animal form (as was common of other ancient deities). There are no theophanies in the New Testament such as are found in the Old Testament because God's ultimate theophany appears there—the incarnation of His son, Jesus Christ.

Further along the way, the angel of the Lord stood in a narrow path between two vineyards, with rock walls on either side. While attempting to pass, the donkey pressed so close to the wall that Balaam's foot was crushed against it. Angrily he beat the animal again (22:25). The donkey and rider encountered the angel of the Lord further along the way in a narrow place where there was no room to pass on either side. Unable to continue, the donkey lay down under Balaam, whereupon he beat her furiously with his staff. The Lord opened the donkey's mouth, and she asked Balaam why he had beat her three times (vv. 26–28). Balaam responded that she had made him appear foolish, and he was angry enough to kill her. The donkey reminded Balaam that he had ridden her many times and should know that her behavior was not normal (vv. 29–30).

Attempts to explain a donkey that talked have been numerous.[1] They include a literal miracle (which must not be ruled out if we place no limits on the power of God), a dream, or a vision experienced by Balaam in the night. Some scholars point out that the text does not actually say the animal spoke with human sounds. Therefore, the painful cries in response to her beating may have been understood as words by Balaam through the "still small voice" of his conscience or by the "inward spiritual ear." However Balaam experienced communication with the donkey, he became convinced that the animal's behavior was unusual.

At that moment the Lord opened Balaam's eyes (literally, "uncovered the eyes of Balaam"), and he saw the angel of the Lord for the first time. In fear he fell face down on the ground (22:31). The angel chided him for beating the donkey. He informed Balaam that He was opposing him because what he was doing was "reckless" ("perverse," KJV; "contrary," NASB; the exact meaning of the Hebrew word is uncertain). He added that because the donkey had seen Him and turned away, Balaam had been spared (vv. 32–33). Balaam acknowledged his sin and his willingness to go back home (v. 34). The angel permitted him to continue the journey after warning Balaam that he must speak only what the angel told him (22:35; cf. Amos 3:8; Jer. 20:9).

5. Balaam's meeting with Balak (22:36–40)

Balak went out to meet Balaam at a Moabite town on the border of Moab that was formed by the Arnon River. He rebuked the diviner for not coming sooner. With the memory of his encounter with the angel of the Lord fresh in his mind, Balaam told the king that he could speak only what God put in his mouth (22:36–38; cf. 1 Kings 22:14). The two men went to Kiriath Huzoth (location unknown), where Balak offered sacrifices (22:40).

B. The oracles of Balaam (22:41–24:25)

1. The first oracle about Israel (22:41–23:12)

The next morning Balak escorted Balaam up to Bamoth Baal (or "the high places of Baal," KJV, NASB, if not a proper name), where he could see the Israelites (22:41). Balaam instructed Balak to build seven altars

---

[1]The discussion by C. F. Keil and Franz Delitzsch, *The Pentateuch, Vol. III,* Biblical Commentary on the Old Testament (Grand Rapids: William B. Eerdmans Publishing Co., 1959 reprint), pp. 168–74, is most helpful.

there and to prepare seven bulls and seven rams for sacrifice. The two
men then offered a bull and a ram on each altar, perhaps to gain God's
favor (23:1–2). Balaam excused himself to go apart to receive a word
from the Lord. God did meet with him and gave him a message to take
back to Balak (vv. 3–5).

Balaam repeated the "oracle" ("parable," KJV; "discourse," RSV;
"poem," JB; the same word is translated "proverbs" in Prov. 1:1) to
Balak and the princes of Moab. He recalled that Balak had sent for him
from Aram (another name for Syria) to curse Israel (23:7). But he
discovered that he could not curse a people whom God had not cursed
(v. 8). Instead, he blessed the people who did "not consider themselves
one of the nations" (v. 9; i.e., they were an elect people, Exod. 19:5).
They were numberless like the dust of the earth (cf. Gen. 13:16; 28:14),
and Balaam wanted to die like a true Israelite ("the death of the right-
eous," 23:10; the phrase should not be interpreted as an allusion to
eternal life).

Balak was furious with Balaam's oracle. He reminded him that he
had been summoned to curse the Israelites, not to bless them. Balaam
responded that he could only speak the words that the Lord put in his
mouth (23:11–12).

2. The second oracle about Israel (23:13–26)

Balak was persistent and asked the diviner to accompany him to
another place where he could curse the Israelites. The two men went
to the field of Zophim on the top of Pisgah (23:13–14). The exact site is
unknown, but it would have overlooked the Jordan Valley and the
plains of Moab, where the Israelites were encamped and could be
seen. Altars were built again, and animals were sacrificed as before
(23:14; cf. 23:1). Again Balaam excused himself to meet the Lord. On
receiving the Lord's message, he returned to Balak and the princes of
Moab and repeated it to them (23:15–17).

Balaam's second oracle was even stronger than the first. Not only did
he refuse to curse Israel, but he expressed support for them and for
their God. He informed Balak that God was not a man (the parallel
phrase "son of man" here only means "a human being") that He would
lie or change His mind ("repent," KJV; the Hebrew word does not
suggest that a mistake has been made and admitted; it expresses only
the emotion of deep sorrow). Whatever He promised, He would do
(23:19). It was obvious to Balaam that God was with Israel. "The shout

of the King is among them" is a reference to God in their midst but contains messianic implications (v. 21).

Balaam recalled Israel's deliverance from Egypt and compared her strength (i.e., victory over enemies) to the strength of a wild ox (23:22; "unicorn," KJV). He admitted that it was impossible to practice sorcery against such a people (v. 23; this verse has also been interpreted to mean that Israel did not practice sorcery). He closed by comparing her to the lion that will not rest until it devours its prey and drinks the blood of its victims (23:24; cf. Gen. 49:9; Deut. 33:20; Mic. 5:8).

Balak was so angry with Balaam's oracle that he ordered him not to speak again about Israel—either to curse or to bless them. Balaam reminded the Moabite ruler that he could only do what the Lord told him to do (23:25–26).

3. The third oracle about Israel (23:27–24:13)

Balak tried once more to use the services of Balaam. By taking him to another place, he hoped God would permit the diviner to curse the Israelites (23:27). They went to the top of Peor (location unknown), and for the third time altars were built and animals sacrificed (vv. 29–30). Balaam now realized that the Lord was pleased when he blessed Israel; so he did not resort to sorcery as he ordinarily did (24:1). As he looked down on the Israelite encampment, the Spirit of God came on him, and he spoke his third oracle (v. 2). The diviner seems now to have become a willing mouthpiece of the Lord.

Balaam acknowledged that his eyes had been opened, and he now saw clearly. He heard the words of God and saw a vision from the Almighty (Hebrew, *Shaddai*, a name for God found forty-eight times in the Old Testament; from a word that means "mountain" or "devastating power"; cf. Exod. 6:3). He looked at the Israelites' tents below him and praised their beauty (24:5). He compared them to fertile valleys and gardens beside a river or flourishing trees (v. 6; the "aloes" is an exotic, aromatic tree, not indigenous to Palestine).

Balaam foresaw a king among them who would be greater than Agag (24:7; "Gog," LXX). The reference to Agag is difficult to explain, as he appeared much later (1 Sam. 15:8–9, 32–33), unless it was a title of Amalekite kings, like Pharaoh (cf. also Esth. 3:1). Again he compared their strength to that of a wild ox and a lion (24:8–9; cf. 23:22, 24; Gen. 49:9). Balaam concluded his oracle by pronouncing a blessing on those who blessed Israel and a curse on those who cursed her (24:9; cf. Gen. 12:3; 27:29).

Balak was so angry with Balaam that he struck his hands together (a gesture of contempt or derision) and ordered him to go home at once (24:10–11). He reminded the diviner that he had planned to pay him well, but the Lord prevented it (literally, "kept you back from honor"). Once again Balaam defended himself by reminding the Moabite ruler that no amount of money could induce him to speak words the Lord had not given him (v. 13).

4. Other oracles (24:14–25)

Balaam departed to return to his people, but not before he had delivered a gratuitous oracle on the coming fate of Moab at the hands of the Israelites. His fourth oracle began with almost the same words as the third (24:15–16; cf. vv. 3–4). He added that he had knowledge from the "Most High" (Hebrew, *Elyon*, a name for God found thirty-one times in the Old Testament; an Aramaic word translated "Most High" appears ten times in the Old Testament, all in Daniel).

In a remarkable oracle, Balaam spoke about a future ruler of Israel ("I see him, but not now"). He called him a "star" that "will come out of Jacob" (literally, "has come out of Jacob"; the form of the verb is called a prophetic perfect or perfect of certainty in Hebrew grammar; it is used to describe a future event as though it had already happened). A star was a well-known metaphor for a great ruler. By Christian times it had become a messianic symbol (cf. Isa. 14:12, where the ruler has fallen; Matt. 2:2; Rev. 22:16). In a parallel statement he called him a "scepter" that "will rise out of Israel" (24:17). Balaam predicted that this ruler was going to crush the Moabites and the sons of Sheth (perhaps "Sutu," a nomadic tribe that dwelt in Palestine, or "sons of strife," NEB; but more likely it is an unexplainable synonym for Moab).

Balaam concluded by speaking a number of unrelated oracles against various peoples. The prediction of subjugation was extended to include Edom (24:18; the parallel word "Seir" was the chief mountain range of Edom and a synonym for that nation; cf. Judg. 5:4). God's enemies were going to become His subjects. Some have interpreted 24:19 to mean political dominion by Israel and destruction of all those who oppose her. The verse has also been understood as an expression of universal messianic dominion.

Balaam looked toward the country of the Amalekites, which could have been visible from the Moabite hills, and called them "first among the nations" (24:20). As the Amalekites were never a great world power, the phrase may mean that they were the first to attack Israel (Exod. 17:8), a choice nation, or an ancient people. However, in the end these descendants of Esau (cf. Gen. 36:12) would come to ruin (cf. 1 Sam. 15:7; 30:1–20).

Balaam then looked toward the land of the Kenites (a tribe of the Sinai Peninsula), which may have been visible from the Moabite hills. They were related to Moses' father-in-law (cf. Judg. 1:16) and at one time were associated with the Amalekites (cf. 1 Sam. 15:6). They were on friendly terms with Judah (cf. Judg. 5:24; 1 Sam 27:10), and it is uncertain as to why they were included in a context of condemnation. Though they were secure ("your nest is set in a rock," cf. Obad. 3–4; Jer. 49:16), yet the Kenites ("Kain," RSV; the spelling in Hebrew is the same as that of Adam's eldest son) would be destroyed. They would be led into captivity by Asshur (24:22; either Assyria, or a local tribe, such as the Asshurites of Genesis 25:3).

Balaam's final oracle is the most obscure of them all (24:23–24). The translation of the Hebrew is uncertain, and there is no known historical event to which it can be linked. Balaam warned that it seemed impossible that anyone could survive the coming catastrophe. Ships were going to come from Kittim (i.e., Cyprus; but the word has also been used of the Mediterranean countries in general, of Rome, and of Greece). They would subdue Asshur and Eber (the latter is translated as "Hebrews," LXX; however, the meaning of Eber in this context is uncertain).

With Balaam's oracles completed, Balaam and Balak went their separate ways (24:25).

For Further Study

1. In a Bible dictionary or encyclopedia (see bibliography) read articles on Moab, Edom, Amalekites, Kenites, and Asshur.

2. Make a study of the various names for God found in the Old Testament.

3. Make a study of beliefs about blessings and curses in the ancient Near East.

4. Make a study of divination as it was practiced in the ancient world.

Chapter 8

A Second Census and Other Regulations
(Numbers 25:1–30:16)

A census was taken at Mount Sinai of the Israelites who had escaped from Egypt. Now, almost forty years later, that generation was dead. A new generation of Israelites was ready to possess the land that had been promised to Abraham and his descendants centuries earlier. There were still things to be done before they could exchange their nomadic existence for settled life on Canaanite soil. A new census was needed to determine their numerical strength. A successor to Moses had not yet been appointed. Regulations governing public worship and other matters of daily life required clarification.

A. Consequences of foreign entanglements (25:1–18)

1. *Apostasy at Peor* (25:1–5)

While the people were encamped at Shittim (literally, "the acacia trees"; probably modern Tell el-Kefrein, ten miles from Jericho and east of the Jordan River), the men began to commit sexual immorality with the Moabite women (25:1). The women invited them to participate in the sacrifices to their gods (v. 2; the chief Moabite deity was named Chemosh). The Israelites shared in the sacred feasts honoring the Moabite deities (in violation of Exod. 20:3). They were introduced for the first time to the worship of Baal of Peor. *Ba'al* is a word that means "lord" or "owner" and is also a Hebrew word for "husband" (e.g., Deut. 24:4). Baal was a fertility god who was worshiped in different localities (such as Peor) as the giver of fertility, the provider of rain, and the insurer of abundant harvests. His worship was accompanied by religious ritual prostitution and unrestrained festivity.

God was angry with His people and ordered that the leaders of the apostasy be killed and that their bodies be disposed of publicly (25:4; cf. 2 Sam. 21:6, 9). The exact mode of execution is not known, as the meaning of the Hebrew word is uncertain. Perhaps death was by hanging (KJV), exposure (NIV), impaling (JB), or throwing over a cliff (NEB). Moses ordered the judges (leaders of tribal groups who settled disputes among their people, Exod. 18:25–26) to slay those of their tribe who had participated in the worship of Baal (25:5).

Balaam is not mentioned in these verses, and at the close of chapter 24 he apparently returned to his own home without cursing Israel. However, 31:16 implies that before departing, he suggested to the Moabite leaders that an effective way of ensnaring the Israelites was to entice them to worship Baal. The consequences of Baal worship for Israel were more disastrous than any curse Balaam might have pronounced. It eventually brought about the destruction of the nation.

2. *The zeal of Phinehas* (25:6–18)

One Israelite boldly brought a Midianite woman into the midst of the congregation, even while they were weeping in front of the Tent of Meeting (25:6). Whether he brought her to marry her or to commit adultery with her, the camp was defiled by the presence of a pagan. Eleazar's son, Phinehas (an Egyptian name that means "Negro"), took a spear and killed the man and the woman in the man's tent (vv. 7–8). The word for "tent" is a *hapax legomenon* (i.e., the word occurs only one time in the Bible); therefore, some think it refers to the inner room of the tabernacle. The plague that was afflicting them stopped, but not before 24,000 died (25:9; cf. Ps. 106:30–31; in 1 Cor. 10:8 the number is 23,000).

The Lord commended Phinehas because he was "zealous" (25:11; "jealous," RSV; cf. comments on 11:29) for the honor of God. God made a "covenant of peace" (a covenant of friendship) with him that assured Phinehas and his descendants of a permanent priesthood (25:12–13; cf. Ezek. 34:25; 37:26; Mal. 2:5; 1 Mac. 2:26). In later times the Zadokite priests claimed their descent from Eleazar through Phinehas (1 Chron. 6:4–8, 50–53; 24:3; Ezra 7:1–6). Phinehas' deed is significant because it apparently resulted in limiting the priesthood to one family, whereas earlier it seems to have been given to the whole tribe of Levi (cf. Exod. 32:27–29; Jer. 33:21; Ezek. 44:10–16; Mal. 2:4, 8).

The offenders in the tragedy were Zimri of the tribe of Simeon and Cozbi (her name means "deceiver") of an important Midianite family

(25:14–15). The Lord gave Moses additional commands concerning the Midianites. They were to be treated as enemies and put to death whenever possible because of their part in the tragedy at Peor (vv. 17–18; cf. their earlier friendship, 10:29).

B. The second census (26:1–65)

1. *Plans for the census* (26:1–4)

After the plague the Lord ordered another census of Israel to be taken on the plains of Moab (cf. chap. 1). Like the first, it was a military census of those twenty years old or more who were fit for military service (26:2). There must have been helpers as before (cf. 1:5–16), but they are not mentioned this time.

2. *The census taken by tribes* (26:5–51)

The census was taken by tribes as before, but in this census a list of clans of each tribe is also recorded. The order in which the tribes are listed is the same, except this time Manasseh appears before Ephraim. Five tribes are now smaller in number (Reuben, Simeon, Gad, Ephraim, and Naphtali). Simeon, the third largest tribe in the first census, is now the smallest of the twelve (26:14; perhaps because of Zimri's sin; cf. 25:6, 14). Seven tribes are larger in number (Judah, Issachar, Zebulun, Manasseh, Benjamin, Dan, and Asher). The greatest increases were registered by Manasseh, Asher, and Benjamin. In both censuses Judah was the largest tribe. The total number of men eligible for military service was approximately the same as before. This time there were 601,730 (26:51), a total decrease of only 1,820 from the first census (1:46). The nation had not decreased in size appreciably, but at the same time it had not experienced a natural growth that would have been expected over a forty-year period.

Reference is made in 26:9–11 to the rebellion of Dathan and Abiram (cf. 16:1, 12). The text adds that not all the family of Korah was destroyed in his rebellion as 16:32 seems to imply (26:11; cf. 1 Chron. 26:1–9, 19; Pss. 42–49).

3. *Regulations for land inheritance* (26:52–56)

The census established the military strength of the tribes, and it was also used as the basis for the division of the land. The larger tribes were to receive a larger portion of land than the smaller tribes (26:52–54). Exact geographical designations and divisions within each tribal area were determined by lot (26:55). This passage agrees with Judges 1:1–3, which suggests that Moses made the division before the tribes actually entered Canaan. However, Joshua 14:1–5; 18:3–10 say that lots were not cast until after Joshua became the leader. The passages can be harmonized by understanding that the command to divide the land was given to Moses but was actually carried out by Joshua (cf. Josh. 17:3–4).

The casting of lots was a common means of settling all kinds of matters in the ancient world (cf. Lev. 16:7–10; Josh. 7:14; 1 Sam. 10:20–21; 14:42; 1 Chron. 24:5; 25:8; 26:13; Neh. 10:34; Prov. 16:33; 18:18; Joel 3:3; Jonah 1:7; Nah. 3:10; Mark 15:24; Acts 1:24–26). The casting of lots seems to have had divine approval as it was done "in the presence of the LORD our God" (Josh. 18:6, 8). Witchcraft was condemned, but the lot was not (Deut. 18:10–12).

4. Census of the Levites (26:57–62)

As in the first census, the Levites were counted separately from the other tribes (26:57; cf. 1:47; 3:14–43). The three main clans of 26:57 are the same as those in 3:17. It is not stated to which of the three clans of 26:57 the Levites of 26:58 belonged (cf. 3:18–20; Exod. 6:16–25 for a more complete list). The family of Kohath is described in greater detail than the others, probably because it was the family to which Moses and Aaron belonged (26:58–61). Jochebed, Moses' mother, is mentioned by name only one other time in the Old Testament (cf. Exod. 6:20). The total number of Levites had increased by one thousand to 23,000 (26:62; cf. 3:39).

5. The only survivors of the desert (26:63–65)

The reader is reminded that none of those counted in the first census were alive when the second was taken, except Caleb and Joshua. God's punishment had been completed (cf. 14:30).

C. Inheritance laws for daughters (27:1–11)

Zelophehad of the tribe of Manasseh died during the desert wanderings, leaving five daughters but no sons (27:1; cf. 26:33). The laws of inheritance of the land apparently gave the right of inheritance only to sons (cf. Deut. 25:5–10). If there were no legal heirs, the land would be given to someone else, and the deceased's family name would disappear from his clan (cf. 2 Sam. 18:18). With this concern in mind,

Zelophehad's daughters went to Moses and asked for their father's property. They reminded Moses that their father had not been among Korah's rebels (27:2–4).

Moses did not pronounce his own judgment but sought a divine ruling (27:5). The Lord approved the daughters' petition and told Moses to give them their father's property (vv. 6–7). He also announced a general law that would apply in similar cases in the future. The inheritance of a man who died without sons would be given to his daughters (v. 8). If he had no daughter, the inheritance would be given to his brothers (v. 9); if he had no brothers, it was to be given to his father's brothers (v. 10). If the father had no brothers, then the inheritance would pass to the nearest surviving relative (v. 11). The purpose of the law was to prevent family land from passing into other hands. It also showed just how important the inheritance was to an Israelite family (cf. Naboth and his vineyard, 1 Kings 21).

D. Appointment of Joshua as Moses' successor (27:12–23)

Moses' time of leadership was rapidly coming to a close. The Lord instructed him to go to the top of a mountain in the Abarim Range (defined as the top of Pisgah, Deut. 3:27, and more specifically as Mount Nebo, Deut. 32:49; 34:1). There he would be allowed to look across the Jordan and see the land God had given to Israel. Afterward, he would die, as Aaron had, for his sin at Meribah in the Desert of Zin (27:12–14; repeated in Deut. 32:48–52; cf. Num. 20:1–13).

Moses' concern was not for himself but for his people. He asked the Lord, "the God of the spirits of all mankind" (27:16; cf. 16:22), to appoint a successor to lead the people like a shepherd (27:17). The phrase "go out and come in before them" is used of military leadership (cf. KJV of Josh. 14:11; 1 Sam. 18:13–16; 2 Kings 11:9), of general leadership in everyday life (Deut. 28:6; 31:2, KJV), and of immaturity (1 Kings 3:7, KJV). It is derived from the picture of a shepherd leading his flock. Moses feared that Israel, without a proper leader, would be as helpless as sheep without a shepherd (cf. 1 Kings 22:17; Ezek. 34:5–6; Zech. 10:2; 13:7; Mark 6:34; John 10:12; Heb. 13:20; 1 Peter 2:25).

The Lord instructed Moses to take Joshua, "a man in whom is the spirit" (an endowment by God), and lay hands on him before Eleazar and the entire assembly (27:18–19). The laying on of hands symbolized the transfer of office and a solemn blessing. It also identified Moses with Joshua in such a way that the people would be willing to obey the new leader (27:20; cf. Deut. 3:28; 31:7). As Moses' successor, Joshua would have some of his "authority" ("honor," KJV; "dignity," NAB) but not all of it, as Moses' role would remain unique.

Moses had been instructed directly by God, but Joshua would have to go to Eleazar the priest for guidance (27:21). Eleazar would in turn learn God's will for Joshua by inquiring of the Urim. Except here and in 1 Samuel 28:6, the Urim is always mentioned in conjunction with the Thummim (cf. Exod. 28:30). It is impossible to know what they looked like. Perhaps they were two stones kept in the priest's breastpiece. They were used as some kind of sacred lot to determine the Lord's will in a given situation. Moses carried out the transfer of leadership to Joshua, as the Lord had instructed him (27:22–23).

E. Regulations for public worship (28:1–29:40)

These two chapters deal with the sacrifices and religious festivals that were to be observed by Israel as expressions of public worship during the course of a year (cf. Lev. 23:3–44 for many parallels). They included daily, weekly, monthly, and annual observances.

1. Introduction (28:1–2)

The Lord told Moses to command the people to be sure to bring food for the offerings made by fire at the appointed times, "as an aroma pleasing to me" (28:2). The words of the command recall to mind ancient pagan beliefs that the deity actually ate and drank with his worshipers. Thus God used an idiom with which the Israelites were familiar in revealing His will through Moses (cf. comments on 15:10).

2. The daily burnt offering (28:3–8)

Instructions were given for daily burnt offerings of two lambs a year old without defect (28:3; cf. the instructions found in Exod. 29:38–42). One was to be offered in the morning and the other in the evening together with a grain offering of a tenth of an ephah of fine flour (about two quarts) mixed with a fourth of a hin of oil from pressed olives (about one quart; 28:4–5, 8). An accompanying drink offering of a fourth of a hin of a "fermented drink" ("strong wine," KJV; "strong drink," RSV, NEB, JB; "wine," NAB) was to be poured out as an offering to the Lord at the sanctuary (v. 7).

3. *The Sabbath offering* (28:9–10)

The daily burnt offerings were doubled on the Sabbath to distinguish this day from the other days of the week (see also Lev. 23:3).

4. *The New Moon offering* (28:11–15)

At the beginning of the month (the time of the new moon) an even larger burnt offering was required (28:11). It was to be accompanied by larger grain and drink offerings than were required with the daily burnt offerings and was given in addition to them. Also, one male goat was to be presented to the Lord as a sin offering (vv. 12–15).

5. *The Feast of Unleavened Bread* (28:16–25)

The Passover was to be observed on the fourteenth day of the first month of the year (28:16; called Pesach in Judaism). The following seven days were the Feast of Unleavened Bread (today popularly called matzah bread), when they could eat only bread made without yeast (28:17; cf. Lev. 23:5–8). No work was to be done on the first or seventh day of this feast (28:18, 25). The amounts of the burnt offering and the grain offering were fixed (vv. 19–21). In addition, a male goat was to be given as a sin offering (v. 22). These offerings were to be in addition to the regular daily burnt offering and its drink offering (vv. 23–24).

6. *The Feast of Weeks* (28:26–31)

On the day of firstfruits during the Feast of Weeks, an offering of new grain was to be brought to the Lord. It was probably brought on the first day of the Feast of Weeks (called Feast of Harvest, Exod. 23:16; Shevuoth in Judaism, Pentecost in the New Testament; cf. Exod. 34:22; Lev. 23:15–22). Instructions for a burnt offering accompanied by a grain offering and a drink offering were also given (28:27–31). In addition, a male goat to make atonement for the people was to be included. All the animals were to be without defect. These offerings (which were the same as those for the New Moon and the Unleavened Bread festivals) were in addition to the regular burnt offering and its grain offering.

7. *The Feast of Trumpets* (29:1–6)

The three festivals that are described in chapter 29 all occurred in the seventh month (September-October). The first day of the seventh month was the Feast of Trumpets (also known as New Year or Rosh

Hashanah; cf. Lev. 23:23–25). It began with the blowing of the ram's horns (29:1) and included a burnt offering, a grain offering, and a sin offering in addition to the regular daily and monthly offerings (vv. 2–6).

8. *The Day of Atonement* (29:7–11)

The Day of Atonement was observed on the tenth day of the seventh month (cf. Lev. 23:26–32; Heb. 9:7–12, 23–28). Also known as Yom Kippur, it became the most important religious day in Judaism. It was a day of self-denial ("afflict your souls," KJV; probably a reference to fasting). The offerings required were the same as those for the Feast of Trumpets, in addition to the regular burnt offering. The regulations for the Day of Atonement are given in detail in Leviticus 16.

9. *The Feast of Tabernacles* (29:12–38)

The last of the three great festivals of the seventh month began on the fifteenth day and lasted for seven days (cf. Lev. 23:33–44). It is also known as the Feast of Booths (NASB), or in Judaism as Sukkoth. It was a time for pilgrimages and joyous celebration of the harvest and of remembrance of the years spent in the desert. The greatest number of offerings during the year were made during this festival. Thirteen bulls, two rams, and fourteen male lambs a year old, all without defect, were offered the first day along with a prescribed grain offering and sin offering. All this was in addition to the regular burnt offering with its grain offering and drink offering (29:12–16).

Each successive day the number of bulls was decreased by one (29:17, 20, 23, 26, 29, 32). The other offerings were the same as those of the first day. On the eighth day the people assembled and presented another burnt offering with its grain and drink offerings, along with a sin offering. The quantities offered were the same as those given on the first and tenth days of the seventh month. All this was in addition to the regular burnt offering with its grain and drink offering (vv. 36–38). Altogether, during the week, seventy bulls, fourteen rams, ninety-eight lambs, and seven goats were offered, not counting those offered on the eighth day or the regular daily burnt offerings.

10. *Conclusion* (29:39–40)

The chapter closes with a note that in addition to the public sacrifices presented during the various festivals, an individual Israelite could bring whatever he wished to vow or any freewill offering he desired to bring (29:39). Moses obediently repeated all the Lord's instructions to the people (v. 40).

F. The vows of women (30:1–16)

Regulations for vows also are found in Leviticus 5:4–5; 7:16; 27:1–29; Numbers 6:2–21; 15:3; and Deuteronomy 12:11, 17 (cf. 1 Sam. 1:11, 21–23; 14:24; 2 Sam. 15:7–8; Ps. 66:13–15; Mal. 1:14; Matt. 5:33–37). Only in Numbers 30, however, is the validity of women's vows discussed.

The law did not require that vows be made, but when a man made a vow or took some kind of obligation on himself by a pledge, the Lord expected him to do everything that he obligated himself to do (30:2). Most scholars distinguish between a vow as a promise to give something (e.g., Judg. 11:30–31; 1 Sam. 1:11) or to do something for God (e.g., Gen. 28:20–22; Jonah 1:16) and a pledge as a prohibition laid on oneself (e.g., Num. 6:2–21; 1 Sam. 14:24). A few scholars say that the vow was a religious obligation and that the pledge was a secular obligation.

The rest of this chapter sets out regulations governing vows and pledges taken by an unmarried daughter living at home under her father's authority, those taken before or after marriage by a wife, and those taken by a widow or a divorced woman.

If an unmarried woman made a vow or obligated herself by a pledge and her father heard about it but said nothing, the vow or pledge would "stand" (30:3–4; "shall be binding," JB). If the father forbade her to keep the vow or the pledge, it would not stand; and the Lord would release her of any obligation (v. 5).

The same rules governed a married woman (30:6–8). If a woman's husband said nothing on learning of a vow or a pledge she had made before they married, it was valid. If he objected, he could nullify the vow or "rash promise" she had made "thoughtless utterance of her lips," RSV). The Lord would not penalize her in such cases.

Since a widow or a divorced woman (literally, "a driven out woman") was not under a man's authority, she was responsible for carrying out any vows or pledges she had made (30:9).

If a woman already married made a vow or a pledge, it was valid if the husband said nothing upon hearing about it (30:10–11). He could however nullify the vow or the pledge at his discretion, and the Lord would release her from any obligation (v. 12). By his silence the husband tacitly gave consent to his wife's vows or pledges (v. 14). If, however, he later changed his mind and decided to nullify the vow or the pledge, then the guilt rested on him (v. 15). Apparently he was required to voice his objection immediately on hearing about the vow or the pledge.

In addition to revealing much about the position of women in the ancient world, this chapter stresses the importance of keeping one's vows. God does not require vows, but when they are freely made, He expects them to be kept (cf. Deut. 23:21–23; Pss. 22:25; 50:14; 116:14, 18; Eccl. 5:4–6). Jesus rebuked those people who thought of clever ways to avoid their vows (cf. Matt. 15:3–9).

For Further Study

1. In a Bible dictionary or encyclopedia (see bibliography) read articles on Baal, Chemosh, lots, Urim, and inheritance.

2. Make a careful comparative study of the two censuses to determine their similarities and differences.

3. Make a study of each of the religious festivals mentioned in chapters 28–29.

4. Make a study of the biblical teachings on vows.

5. Make a list of the various ways to determine God's will that are found in the Bible.

Chapter 9

The Beginning of the Conquest
(Numbers 31:1–33:56)

Though God had given Canaan to the people of Israel, it did not become theirs in fact without bloody conflicts with the people who already inhabited it. The Israelites had already experienced conflicts with the Amalekites, the Amorites, and others as they made their way toward the Promised Land. The Midianite threat was more subtle but also required military action. The tribes of Gad and Reuben preferred to settle permanently on the eastern side of the Jordan but agreed to help their kinsmen conquer Canaan before returning to the land they chose for their inheritance.

A. War against the Midianites (31:1–54)

1. *Victory over the enemy* (31:1–12)

At the close of chapter 25 the Lord ordered Moses to take vengeance on the Midianites because of what happened at Peor. It was to be Moses' last effort as leader before being gathered to his people (31:2).

Moses called the tribes to arms and requested a thousand troops from each tribe (31:3–4). Phinehas the priest accompanied them into battle (v. 6). His presence may have been required because the effort was considered a "holy war" or because of his previous zeal against the Midianites (see 25:6–13; cf. Josh. 22:13). He took some of the sacred articles from the tabernacle with him (their exact identity is not given; cf. 1 Sam. 4:3–11, where the ark was taken into battle). The trumpets for signaling were also carried into battle (cf. 10:1–10; 2 Chron. 13:12). The Israelites had a great victory over the Midianites. They killed all the enemy soldiers, the five Midianite kings (cf. Josh. 13:21), and also Balaam, who earlier had tried unsuccessfully to curse them (cf. chaps.

22–24). They took women, children, herds, and goods as plunder, and burned the Midianite towns and camps (31:7–10). Then they returned to the Israelite camp on the plains of Moab with their plunder (vv. 11–12).

2. *Extermination of the enemy* (31:13–18)

The victorious Israelites probably expected praise from Moses, but he angrily demanded to know why they let the women live (31:13–15; cf. 1 Sam. 15:18–19). He told them that the Midianite women were responsible for the calamity at Peor and must be killed along with the male children (cf. Judg. 21:11). Only the virgins could be spared to be used as concubines and servants (31:16–18).

The wars of extermination of Israel's enemies that are frequently encountered in the Old Textament (cf. also Deut. 20; sometimes called "holy war" by scholars) remain one of the most disturbing moral questions of the Bible. It is difficult to understand how the God of love who commands us to forgive our enemies and to turn the other cheek could order such wholesale destruction of the native inhabitants of Canaan in order to give their land to the Israelites.

The problem is not easy to solve, but some factors to be taken into consideration include: (1) God's sovereignty; as Creator He can do whatever He desires with what He created and is answerable to no one (cf. Jer. 18:6). Past generations had no difficulty accepting this concept of absolute divine sovereignty. The present generation is probably the first that has not been afraid to question God's sovereignty openly and therefore cannot understand the wars of extermination. (2) God's justice; though He is sovereign, His actions are always just, else He is not worthy of worship. The wars of extermination were God's punishment on the wicked inhabitants of Canaan for their sins (cf. Deut. 9:4–6; 18:12; Rom. 3:23). The Bible indicates that war has been used in history as an agent of God's judgment—even on His own people (e.g., Israel's punishment at the hands of Assyria and Judah's destruction at the hands of Babylonia).

Other factors to be considered are: (3) The seriousness of sin; a generation that is inclined to be soft on sin needs the reminder that God is holy and will punish sin (cf. Lev. 19:2; Rom. 6:23). He is not so ecumenical as many today portray Him, i.e., willing to overlook any offense against Him in order to save everyone. The seriousness of sin is seen in God's determination not to spare even His own Son in order to

deal with sin and to make it possible for the human race to be recon-
ciled to Him. (4) The source of sin; God is not the author of sin. Its
source is the rebellious human heart that refuses to live in submission
to God. Consequently, each one, whether ancient Canaanite or
twentieth-century sophisticate, must be prepared to accept the consequences of sin (cf. Amos 4:12).

3. *Purification of soldiers and spoils* (31:19–24)

The law stated that contact with a corpse made a person ritually
unclean, and the uncleanness had to be removed (cf. chap. 19). Moses
instructed the soldiers who had killed anyone or who had touched a
corpse to remain outside the camp for seven days. They were to purify
themselves and their captives (literally, "unsin yourselves") on the
third and seventh days, as well as their clothing and anything made of
leather, goat hair, or wood (31:19–20). Gold, silver, bronze, iron, tin,
lead, and anything else that could withstand fire was also to be purified
by passing it through fire and then through the water of cleansing (vv.
22–23; cf. 19:9). This particular regulation is not mentioned elsewhere
in the Old Testament. Anything that could not withstand fire was to be
purified by passing it through the water alone (v. 23). On the seventh
day, after washing their clothes, they were clean and could return to
the camp (v. 24).

4. *Division of the spoils* (31:25–54)

The Lord appointed Eleazar and family heads of the community to
assist Moses in counting the people and the animals captured from the
Midianites (31:26). He further instructed them to divide the spoils
equally, with one-half for the soldiers who fought the Midianites and
one-half for the rest of the people (31:27; cf. 1 Sam. 30:21–25, where
David established this division of spoils as a permanent regulation).
From the soldiers' half, they were to set aside one out of every five
hundred people or animals as "tribute" (31:28; "tax," NAB, NEB; this
word occurs only in this chapter in the Old Testament). The tribute
was for the Lord and was to be delivered to Eleazar for the priests' use
(v. 29). One out of fifty of the people's share of the spoils was to be
given as tribute and delivered to the Levites for their use (v. 30). It is
not stated whether the Midianite captives who were given as tribute to
the Lord were put to death or enslaved.

The huge amount of plunder that the soldiers brought back for distribution was carefully enumerated (31:32–35). The number of sheep, cattle, donkeys, and people belonging to the soldiers was also recorded along with the part due to the Lord. The Lord's part was delivered to Eleazar the priest (vv. 36–41). The people's half of the sheep, cattle, donkeys, and people was also enumerated. One out of every fifty persons and animals belonging to them was given to the Levites as the Lord had instructed Moses (vv. 42–47).

The army officers reported to Moses that there had not been a single casualty among the Israelite soldiers (31:48–49).[1] In gratitude, they brought an offering of gold ornaments taken from the bodies of the enemy to make atonement before the Lord (31:50; cf. Judg. 8:24–26). The Hebrew word for "offering" used here is *korban*, a gift that was consecrated to God to be used only for religious purposes (cf. Mark 7:11). Exodus 30:11–16 required that atonement money be brought to the Lord after a census. Thus, the soldiers brought the ornaments as the atonement money because they were probably counted after returning from battle to determine if there had been any losses.

Moses and Eleazar accepted the gold, which weighed 16,750 shekels (estimated between 420–600 pounds), as a memorial before the Lord for the Israelites (31:51–53; "that the Lord might remember Israel," NEB). The gold was probably fashioned into vessels for use in the sanctuary. These items visibly reminded the people of a time when God acted in an unusual way to bring help and deliverance.

B. The request of Reuben and Gad (32:1–42)

1. *The request to remain across the Jordan* (32:1–5)

The tribes of Reuben and Gad, who possessed large herds and flocks, saw that the fertile lands of Jazer and Gilead on the east side of the Jordan were suitable for livestock. They went to Moses, Eleazar, and the other leaders and requested the land as their inheritance, rather than land in Canaan (32:1–5).

2. *Moses' response to the request* (32:6–15)

Moses assumed that they were excusing themselves from fighting with their kinsmen to possess Canaan so he rebuked them. He re-

---

[1]Many scholars dismiss the account of such a one-sided victory as idealistic or legendary. However, many other historical battles have resulted in equally disproportionate casualties. For example, at the Battle of Agincourt on October 25, 1415, the English, outnumbered four to one, slew five thousand Frenchmen and suffered only one hundred casualties.

membered the calamitous consequences when the tribes refused to
enter Canaan at Kadesh (called Kadesh Barnea here for the first time).
He feared the same thing was happening again (32:6-9; cf. 14:29-30).
He recalled the forty years of punishment God had inflicted on them
for that sin (vv. 10-13). In anger he called the Reubenites and Gadites
a "brood of sinners" (v. 14; a term of contempt not found elsewhere in
the Old Testament). He feared they were going to bring a repetition of
God's wrath that would destroy the entire nation (v. 15).

3. *Assurances of Reuben and Gad* (32:16-27)

The tribes of Reuben and Gad quickly assured Moses that they did
not intend to desert their kinsmen in the struggle to take Canaan. They
requested time to build pens for their livestock (probably of heaped-up
stones) and fortified towns in which the women and children could
remain for protection (32:16). The men promised to fight with their
kinsmen until every Israelite received his inheritance in Canaan. Only
then would they return to the east side of the Jordan and establish their
inheritance there (vv. 7-19).

Moses agreed to their request (32:20-22), but warned that if they
failed to keep their word, they were sinning against the Lord. He
solemnly warned them, "Be sure that your sin will find you out" (32:23;
cf. Rom. 6:23). The phrase reflects an ancient belief that sin, like a
curse, had an independent existence; a person could not hide himself
from its consequences (cf. Amos 9:1-4). Again they assured Moses that
they would do as they had agreed. Their families and livestock would
remain in the cities of Gilead while they crossed over the Jordan with
the other tribes to fight alongside them (32:25-27).

4. *Moses' consent to the request* (32:28-32)

Moses informed Eleazar, Joshua, and leaders of the tribes of the
request of the Reubenites and Gadites, as he knew he would not live to
see whether they kept their word. He instructed the other tribes to
allow Reuben and Gad to take Gilead as their inheritance if they fought
with their kinsmen to take Canaan. Otherwise, they would be obligated to accept their inheritance in Canaan with the other tribes
(32:28-30).

5. *Settlement of land apportioned to them* (32:33-42)

Moses then gave the territory of Sihon and Og with all its cities to the Gadites, Reubenites, and the half-tribe of Manasseh (32:33; cf. 21:21-35). This is the first mention of Manasseh sharing in the land east of the Jordan. The tradition that Moses included Manasseh in the distribution of the Trans-Jordanian land is found elsewhere, also (Deut. 3:12-14; 4:43; 29:7-8; Josh. 12:6; 13:29, 31; 14:3; 18:7).

The Gadites took possession of eight towns, built up their fortifications, and constructed pens for their flocks (32:34-36; cf. v. 3). The Reubenites took possession of six towns, rebuilt them, and renamed them (32:37-38; cf. Josh. 13:15-32 for an even larger list of towns belonging to the Trans-Jordanian tribes). The locations of most of the fourteen towns named in these verses are known. They are situated in an area bounded on the north by the Jabbok River, on the south by the Arnon, and on the west by the Jordan River and the Dead Sea. (A map and an up-to-date Bible dictionary should be consulted for additional information about each of these towns.)

The remaining verses of the chapter contain an account of the capture of territory east of the Jordan by three Manassite clans (32:39-42). The descendants of Manasseh's son Makir (Machir, KJV, RSV) took Gilead and drove out the Amorites who lived there (cf. 26:29). Jair, Makir's great-grandson, took some of their villages and called them Havvoth Jair (i.e., "settlements of Jair"; cf. 1 Chron. 2:21-23). Nobah, presumably a Manassite also, though he is not mentioned elsewhere, took Kenath and its surrounding settlements and renamed it for himself (1 Chron. 2:23 retains the name Kenath, though there is a Nobah mentioned in Judg. 8:11).

C. A review of Israel's journey (33:1-56)

1. *Introduction* (33:1-2)

As the journey from Egypt neared its end, it was appropriate that a summary of the journey be recalled. It would be impossible to trace the route the Israelites followed from Egypt to the plains of Moab from the information given in this chapter because the location of many of the encampments is unknown. A number of them are not mentioned elsewhere in the Bible. Some encampments mentioned elsewhere are not found in this list (e.g., Massah, Meribah, Taberah). Moses recorded the stages in their journey (33:2).

2. *From Rameses to Sinai* (33:3-15)

On the day following the first Passover the journey began at

Rameses, one of the cities the enslaved Hebrews had built for the Pharaoh. They marched out "boldly" ("with an high hand," KJV; cf. comment on 15:30) while the Egyptians were burying their firstborn who had been killed by the tenth plague (33:3–4; cf. Exod. 12:37). The route described in 33:3–15 corresponds to Exodus 12:37–19:1. All the places named are found in both passages except Dophkah and Alush, which are mentioned only in 33:12–14. (For additional information on each of the encampments named, an up-to-date Bible dictionary and commentaries on Exodus should be consulted.) The events that occurred during the time spent at Sinai (v. 15) are elaborated in Exodus 19:2–Numbers 10:10.

3. From Sinai to Kadesh (33:16–36)

After encamping at Sinai for more than eleven months, the Israelites resumed their journey. The route described in 33:16–36 is paralleled in 10:11–12:16 by a fuller account of events along the way. Thirteen places named in 33:16–36 are not mentioned elsewhere in the Old Testament; therefore, it is impossible to trace the exact route the Israelites followed from Sinai to Kadesh. The problem is compounded by lingering uncertainty about the location of Mount Sinai.

4. From Kadesh to Mount Hor (33:37–40)

After refusing to enter the Promised Land at Kadesh, the Israelites were forced to live nomadic lives for almost forty years. The route described in 33:37–40 is paralleled in 13:1–21:3 by a fuller account of events along the way. Near the end of the wanderings, Aaron died at the age of 123 (cf. Exod. 7:7).

5. From Mount Hor to the plains of Moab (33:41–49)

The route described in 33:41–49 is paralleled in 21:4–22:1 by accounts of some things that happened during the final stage of the journey on the way to the plains of Moab. The Israelites encamped along the Jordan from Beth Jeshimoth to Abel Shittim awaiting the command to enter Canaan (33:49).

6. Instructions concerning the conquest of Canaan (33:50–56)

The Lord instructed Moses to command the Israelites to drive out the Canaanite inhabitants and to destroy all their idols and places of worship (33:50–52; cf. Deut. 12:2–3). The instructions for the division of the land by lot among the tribes were repeated (33:54; cf. 26:54–56).

Moses also warned the Israelites that if they failed to drive out the native inhabitants, those remaining would become like "barbs in your eyes and thorns in your sides" (33:55; cf. Josh. 23:13; Ezek. 28:24; 2 Cor. 12:7). They would be a constant source of irritation and vexation to the Israelites if allowed to remain. If Israel failed to drive out the Canaanites as commanded, the punishment intended for the Canaanites would fall on Israel (33:56). This fate finally overtook them because they did not drive out the Canaanites but settled among them and even began to worship their gods (cf. Hos. 11:2; Jer. 2:28; Ezek. 6:13). They refused to heed the warnings of the prophets to give up their idols and turn back to God. The Lord was long-suffering and patient with His people for centuries after they occupied Canaan; but when all warnings failed, judgment finally overtook them. Israel was conquered by Assyria in 722 B.C., and Judah was taken by the Babylonians in 587 B.C.

For Further Study

1. In a Bible dictionary or encyclopedia (see bibliography) read articles on Midian and Corban.

2. Make a study of warfare in the ancient Near East, especially the concept of "holy war."

3. With the help of maps and a Bible dictionary, study the route taken by the Israelites described in chapter 33.

Chapter 10

Further Instructions Before Crossing the Jordan
(Numbers 34:1–36:13)

While the Israelites awaited the signal to begin their invasion of Canaan, the Lord gave them additional regulations to govern them in the Promised Land. Boundaries were clarified, cities of refuge were established, and the laws governing women's inheritances were modified.

A. Tribal boundaries in Canaan (34:1–29)

1. *Introduction* (34:1–2)

The Lord designated the boundaries of the land that the Israelites were to occupy in Canaan. A careful study of a map reveals that the territory described in these verses was not fully occupied by Joshua's conquest. The description fits more closely the territory occupied by King David (cf. the boundaries described in Ezek. 47–48).

2. *Description of the boundaries* (34:3–15)

a) *The southern boundary* (34:3–5)

The southern boundary was to begin at the southern end of the Salt Sea (i.e., the Dead Sea). It would turn south of Scorpion Pass ("the ascent of Akrabbim," KJV, RSV) and include part of the Desert of Zin along the border of Edom. Then it would continue south to Kadesh Barnea, westward to Hazar Addar (cf. Josh. 15:3; location unknown), and then to Azmon (location uncertain). From there it would join the Wadi of Egypt and follow it to the Mediterranean Sea (34:3–5; cf. the description in Josh. 15:1–4; Ezek. 47:19). The wadi ("Brook of Egypt," RSV) was not the Nile, but Wadi el-Arish, which rises in the center of the Sinai Peninsula and flows northward into the Mediterranean about fifty miles southwest of Gaza.

b) *The western boundary* (34:6)

The coast of the Great Sea (i.e., the Mediterranean; also called "the sea," e.g., Josh. 16:8; 1 Kings 5:9; cf. Ezek. 47:20) was to serve as the western boundary. The Philistines occupied the area between Judah and the Mediterranean throughout the monarchy, but David subdued them during his reign (2 Sam. 8:1). Hezekiah occupied their territory for a short time (2 Kings 18:8). The sea did not actually become Israel's boundary until the Maccabean occupation of Joppa in the second century B.C.

c) *The northern boundary* (34:7–9)

The northern boundary is more difficult to trace because it was to begin at a site on the Mediterranean that cannot be identified (34:7; cf. Ezek. 47:15–17). From there it would go eastward to Mount Hor (otherwise unknown, but not the Mount Hor of 20:22, which was near the border of Edom). Then it would continue to Lebo Hamath ("entrance of Hamath," KJV, RSV), near the head of the Orontes River. It would pass through Zedad (i.e., Sadad, between Palmyra and Riblah), through Ziphron (location uncertain), and terminate at Hazar Enan (perhaps modern Qaryatein).

d) *The eastern boundary* (34:10–12)

The eastern boundary was to begin at Hazar Enan and continue southwest to Shepham (location unknown) to Riblah (unknown; not Riblah on the Orontes). It would continue along the east side of the Sea of Kinnereth (which means "harp-shaped"; "Chinnereth," KJV, RSV; Gennesaret or the Sea of Galilee in the New Testament). From there it would go south along the Jordan to the Dead Sea (cf. Ezek. 47:18).

e) *The Trans-Jordanian tribes* (34:13–15)

Without specifically describing the boundaries of the tribes who chose to remain on the east side of the Jordan, the reader is reminded in these verses that the land of Canaan was to be divided among nine and one-half tribes. Reuben, Gad, and the half-tribe of Manasseh received their inheritance across the Jordan.

3. *The officials in charge of the land division* (34:16–29)

The Lord instructed Moses to appoint Eleazar, Joshua, and one leader from each tribe to help in the division of the land (34:16–18). Of the tribal leaders named, only Caleb is familiar (vv. 19–29; cf. the description of the land division in Josh. 13–19). The order of the tribes here seems to be governed by their geographical location in Canaan.

The four southern tribes are listed first (34:19–22), followed by the one and a half central tribes (vv. 23–24), and finally the four northern tribes (vv. 25–28).

B. The Levitical cities (35:1–34)

The Levites did not share in the division of the land, so they were assigned special cities to live in. Because of the Hebrew passion for justice, other cities were set aside to which persons accused of murder could flee. There the accused could safely remain until it was determined whether or not he were guilty. Chapter 35 gives the regulations that governed the cities of refuge (cf. Josh. 20–21 for the carrying out of these measures; also cf. Ezek. 48:8–14).

1. *Designation of the cities* (35:1–8)

The Lord commanded that towns be given to the Levites from the inheritance of the other tribes as well as pasturelands around the towns for their livestock (35:1–3). Dimensions for the amount of pastureland around each city were also specified (vv. 4–5). According to Joshua 21, the priests received thirteen cities from Judah, Simeon, and Benjamin. The Kohathites were allocated ten cities by Ephraim, Dan, and the half-tribe of Manasseh west of the Jordan. The Gershonites were given thirteen cities by Issachar, Asher, Naphtali, and the half-tribe of Manasseh east of the Jordan. The Merarites were given twelve cities by Reuben, Gad, and Zebulun.

In all, the Levites were to be given forty-eight towns, six of which were designated as cities of refuge (see Josh. 20:7–8 for the names of the cities of refuge; cf. Deut. 4:41–43; 19:2, 9). A person who had killed someone or who was accused of killing someone could flee there for protection from a miscarriage of justice (35:6–7). The towns were to be contributed by each tribe in proportion to the size of that tribe (v. 8).

2. *The cities of refuge* (35:9–28)

The cities of refuge provided protection for any person, whether Israelite or resident alien (cf. comments on 9:14), who killed someone accidentally. The law of "eye for eye" (Exod. 21:24; called *lex talionis*, or the law of retaliation) did not distinguish between accidental and intentional killing. The law of refuge did. The accused was safe from the avenger[1] (the nearest kinsman of the deceased). He could not be executed until he stood trial before the assembly (35:11–12). Deuteronomy 19:12 suggests the judges were elders of the accused's own town. Numbers 35:25 implies that judgment took place somewhere other than in the city of refuge, perhaps in the accused's own town. If the accused were found guilty, he was handed over to the avenger. To make it easier for an accused man to find refuge, half of the cities of refuge were to be on either side of the Jordan (v. 14).

The right of asylum did not extend to a man who murdered deliberately. Criteria were established to determine if the murder was willful. If a man killed another by striking him with an iron object or with a stone or wooden object in his hand, he was adjudged a murderer and sentenced to die (35:16–19). Apparently the person who conveniently had one of these objects available was deemed to have murderous intents when he encountered the victim. Also if he pushed him ("stabbed him," RSV), threw something at him intentionally, or hit him with his fist out of hatred, and the man died, the murderer was to be sentenced to die (vv. 20–21). The kinsman-avenger was to be the executioner (vv. 19, 21), in contrast to capital punishment today which is carried out by the state.

Hebrew justice recognized that accidental killing should be dealt with differently from premeditated murder. Therefore, if a person without hostile intent shoved ("stabbed," RSV) someone, threw something at him unintentionally, or dropped a stone on him without seeing him, and the person died, the assembly was required to protect the accused from the avenger (35:22–25). After judging that the deed was accidental, the assembly was required to send the accused back to the city of refuge to which he had fled. There he had to remain until the death of the high priest (v. 25; literally, "the great priest"). His detention in the city of refuge served as his punishment.

The one who killed unintentionally was not totally absolved from the crime; for not only was he restricted to the city of refuge, but he also could be put to death by the avenger if he left the city (35:26–27). Only

---

[1]The Mosaic law placed five obligations on the avenger or kinsman-redeemer (Hebrew, *go'el*): (1) to avenge the blood of a murdered relative (Num. 35:19); (2) to marry the widow of a brother who died without a son (Deut. 25:5–10); (3) to repurchase a brother's property that had been sold (Lev. 25:25); (4) to buy the freedom of a brother who had been sold into slavery (vv. 47–49); and (5) to help a poor and needy brother by providing shelter, food, and money for him (vv. 35–37). Christians see Christ as the divine Kinsman-Redeemer.

after the death of the man who was high priest when the killing occurred could the accused return to his own home safely (v. 28).

3. *The law for murder* (35:29–34)

Further safeguards against miscarriage of justice in the case of murder were also provided. In addition to protection by the tests previously described (35:16–21), the accused could be put to death as a murderer only on the testimony of witnesses (v. 30). The exact number of witnesses is not stated, but at least two are implied (cf. Deut. 17:6; 19:15; Matt. 18:16; 26:59–61; John 8:17–18; 2 Cor. 13:1; Heb. 10:28).

A person found guilty of murder could not buy his freedom by paying a ransom (35:31; cf. Exod. 21:12–14; Deut. 19:1–13; Lev. 24:17), a common practice elsewhere in the ancient world. Not even a person living under the protection of a city of refuge could pay a ransom and then be free to return home before the death of the high priest (35:32). The taking of a life was such a serious offense that no exceptions could be made that would allow a person to escape the penalty due him. Bloodshed polluted the land (cf. Ps. 106:38; Isa. 24:5). The only way that atonement could be made for land on which blood had been shed was by the blood of the one who shed it (35:33; cf. Gen. 4:10; 9:6). Because God Himself lived among His people (35:34), the holiness of God required that atonement be made for Israelite land defiled by bloodshed.

The regulations concerning the cities of refuge teach that (1) justice is rarely achieved in the heat of passion; (2) human life is sacred to God; and (3) violence pollutes a people and a land.

C. The inheritance of women (36:1–12)

The family heads of the clan of Gilead (of the tribe of Manasseh) came to Moses with a problem precipitated by the ruling on the daughters of Zelophehad (36:1; cf. chap. 27). Moses had ruled that, in the absence of sons, the inheritance of Zelophehad should go to his five daughters. The Gileadite leaders foresaw the possibility that the daughters might marry outside their own tribe. If they did, their inheritance would pass to the tribe into which they married because their sons, as heirs, would be considered to be members of the tribe of their father. Therefore, the ruling, the intent of which had been to avoid this very possibility, could be circumvented and in practice would be nullified if women married outside their tribe (36:2–3).

Furthermore, the Gileadites pointed out that even the regulations of the Year of Jubilee (literally, "the ram"; from the custom of blowing a ram's horn to inaugurate the Jubilee) would not keep the land from passing permanently to another tribe (36:4; cf. Lev. 25:8–34). The laws governing the Year of Jubilee required that any family land that had been sold be returned to its original owners or their descendants every fiftieth year. However, this law did not affect cases where land had passed out of the tribe through inheritance by persons of another tribe.

The entire episode concerning Zelophehad's daughters is an interesting case of divine revelation being modified. The Lord instructed Moses to tell the Israelites that the men who had come to him from the clan of Gilead were right (36:5). Therefore, he modified the previous law by stating that Zelophehad's daughters could only marry someone of their own tribe. No inheritance could pass from tribe to tribe (vv. 6–9).

Zelophehad's daughters obeyed this new injunction. They married cousins on their father's side of the family, thus keeping their inheritance in their father's clan and tribe (36:10–12; cf. 1 Chron. 23:22 for a similar case).

D. A final reminder (36:13)

The Book of Numbers closes with a brief subscription that covers the laws and regulations given in the closing chapters, 27–36, of the book (cf. Lev. 27:34).

Some important lessons to be remembered from the Book of Numbers are: (1) God acts for the ultimate good of His people although their experiences along the way may sometimes be painful; (2) God demands that His people obey Him; and (3) God is able to accomplish His purposes in spite of sins that may sometimes delay their accomplishment.

For Further Study

1. In a Bible dictionary or encyclopedia (see bibliography) read articles on witnesses, avenger of blood, ransom, and the Year of Jubilee.

2. Draw the boundaries of Israel on a map as they are described in chapter 34.

3. Make a study of the biblical teachings concerning capital punishment.

4. See if you can recall from memory the principal events in the Book of Numbers.

Bibliography

Commentaries on Numbers

Binns, L. Elliott. *The Book of Numbers with Introduction and Notes* in *Westminster Commentaries*. London: Methuen & Co., Ltd., 1927.

Erdman, Charles R. *The Book of Numbers: An Exposition*. Westwood, N.J.: Fleming H. Revell Co., 1952.

Fisch, S. "The Book of Numbers" in *Soncino Books of the Bible*, vol. 1, pp. 792, 897. Edited by A. Cohen. London: The Soncino Press, 1947.

Gray, George Buchanan. *A Critical and Exegetical Commentary on Numbers*. The International Critical Commentary. Edinburgh: T. & T. Clark, 1903.

Honeycutt, Roy Lee, Jr. *Leviticus, Numbers, Deuteronomy*. Layman's Bible Book Commentary. Nashville: Broadman Press, 1979.

Keil, C. F., and Delitzsch, F. *The Pentateuch*, vol. III. Biblical Commentary on the Old Testament. Grand Rapids: William B. Eerdmans Publishing Co., 1959 reprint.

Kenneday, A. R. S. *Leviticus and Numbers*. Century Bible. Edinburgh: T. C. & E. C. Jack, n.d.

Marsh, John. "The Book of Numbers: Introduction and Exegesis." *The Interpreter's Bible*, vol. 2, pp. 135–308. Edited by George Arthur Buttrick et al. New York/Nashville: Abingdon Press, 1953.

Mays, James L. *The Book of Leviticus; The Book of Numbers*. The Layman's Bible Commentary. Richmond: John Knox Press, 1963.

McNeile, A. H. *The Book of Numbers*. The Cambridge Bible for Schools and Colleges. Cambridge: University Press, 1911.

Noth, Martin. *Numbers*. The Old Testament Library. London: SCM Press, Ltd., 1968.

Owens, John Joseph. "Numbers." *The Broadman Bible Commentary*, vol. 2, pp. 75–174. Edited by Clifton J. Allen et al. Nashville: Broadman Press, 1970.

Snaith, Norman H. *Leviticus and Numbers*. The Century Bible New Edition. London: Thomas Nelson and Sons, Ltd., 1967.

Snaith, Norman H. *Numbers*. Peake's Commentary on the Bible, pp. 254–68. Edited by Matthew Black and H. H. Rowley. London: Thomas Nelson and Sons, Ltd., 1963.

Sturdy, John. *Numbers*. The Cambridge Bible Commentary on the New English Bible. London: Cambridge University Press, 1976.

Thompson, J. A. "Numbers." *The New Bible Commentary Revised*, 3d. ed., pp. 168–200. Edited by D. Guthrie et al. Grand Rapids: William B. Eerdmans Publishing Co., 1970.

Bible Dictionaries and Encyclopedias

Buttrick, George Arthur, ed. *The Interpreter's Dictionary of the Bible*. 4 vols. New York/Nashville: Abingdon Press, 1962.

Douglas, J. D., ed. *The New Bible Dictionary*. Grand Rapids: William B. Eerdmans Publishing Co., 1970.

Crim, Keith, ed. *The Interpreter's Dictionary of the Bible: Supplementary Volume*. Nashville: Abingdon Press, 1976.

Orr, James, ed. *The International Standard Bible Encyclopedia*. 5 vols. William B. Eerdmans Publishing Co., 1957 reprint.

Tenney, Merrill C., ed. *The Zondervan Pictorial Bible Dictionary*, rev. ed. Grand Rapids: Zondervan Publishing House, 1967.

Tenney, Merrill C., ed. *The Zondervan Pictorial Encyclopedia of the Bible*. 5 vols. Grand Rapids: Zondervan Publishing House, 1975.

Unger, Merrill F. *Unger's Bible Dictionary*. Chicago: Moody Press, 1957.

Bible Translations

The Bible: A New Translation by James Moffatt. New York: Harper & Row, Publishers, 1954. Referred to in the Bible Study Commentary as Moffatt.

Good News Bible: The Bible in Today's English Version. New York: American Bible Society, 1976. Referred to in the Bible Study Commentary as TEV.

Jerusalem Bible. Garden City, New York: Doubleday & Co., Inc., 1966. Referred to in the Bible Study Commentary as JB.

King James Version. Referred to in the Bible Study Commentary as KJV.

New American Bible. New York: The World Publishing Co., 1970. Referred to in the Bible Study Commentary as NAB.

New American Standard Bible. La Habra, CA: Foundation Press Publications, 1973. Referred to in the Bible Study Commentary as NASB.

New English Bible. Oxford: Oxford University Press, 1970. Referred to in the Bible Study Commentary as NEB.

New International Version. Grand Rapids: Zondervan Bible Publishers, 1978. Referred to in the Bible Study Commentary as NIV.

Revised Standard Version. New York: Thomas Nelson & Sons, 1953. Referred to in the Bible Study Commentary as RSV.

Septuagint Version of the Old Testament and Apocrypha. Grand Rapids: Zondervan Publishing House, 1972 reprint. Referred to in the Bible Study Commentary as LXX.